MW00826513

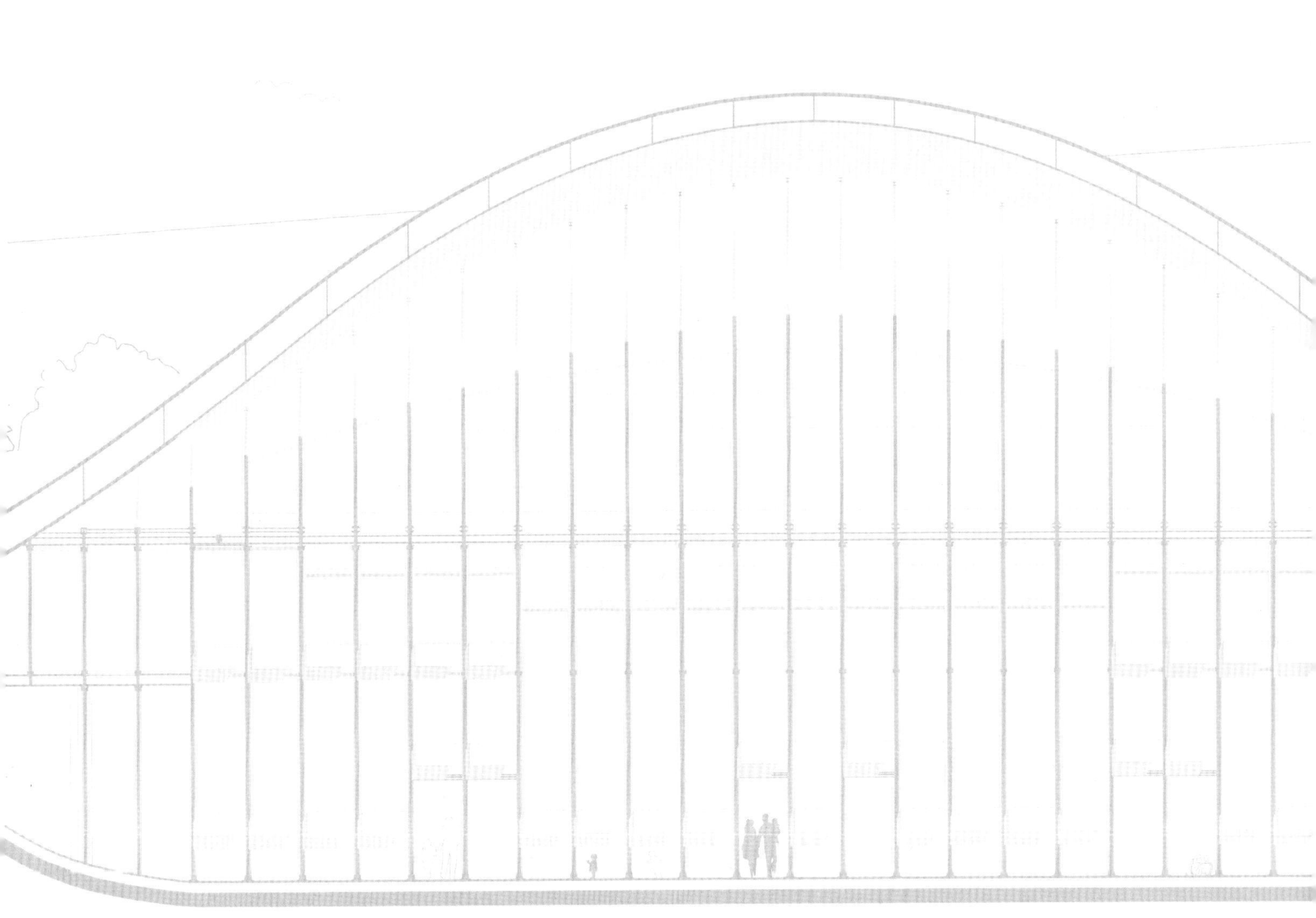

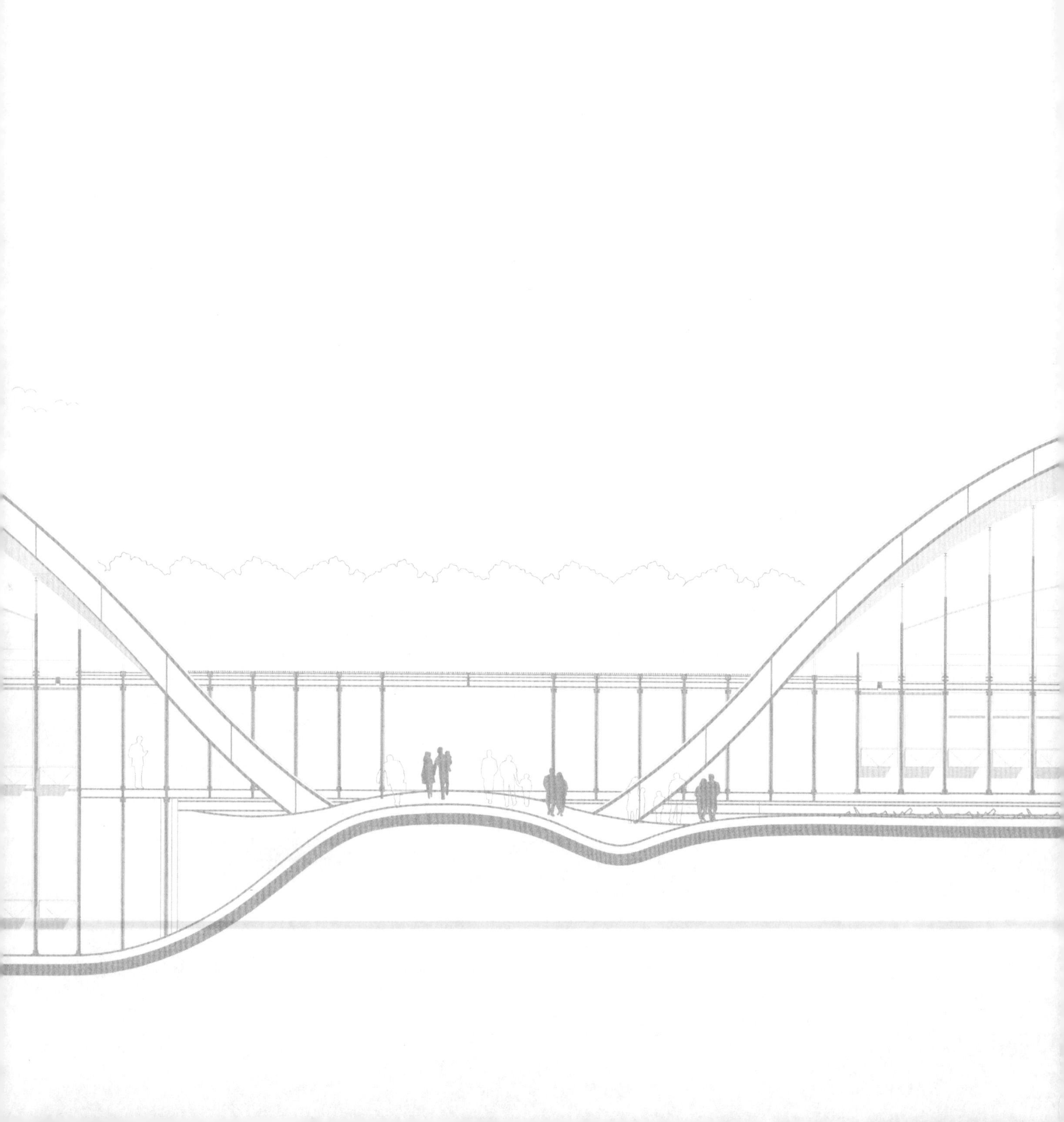

Zentrum Paul Klee, Bern

The Architecture

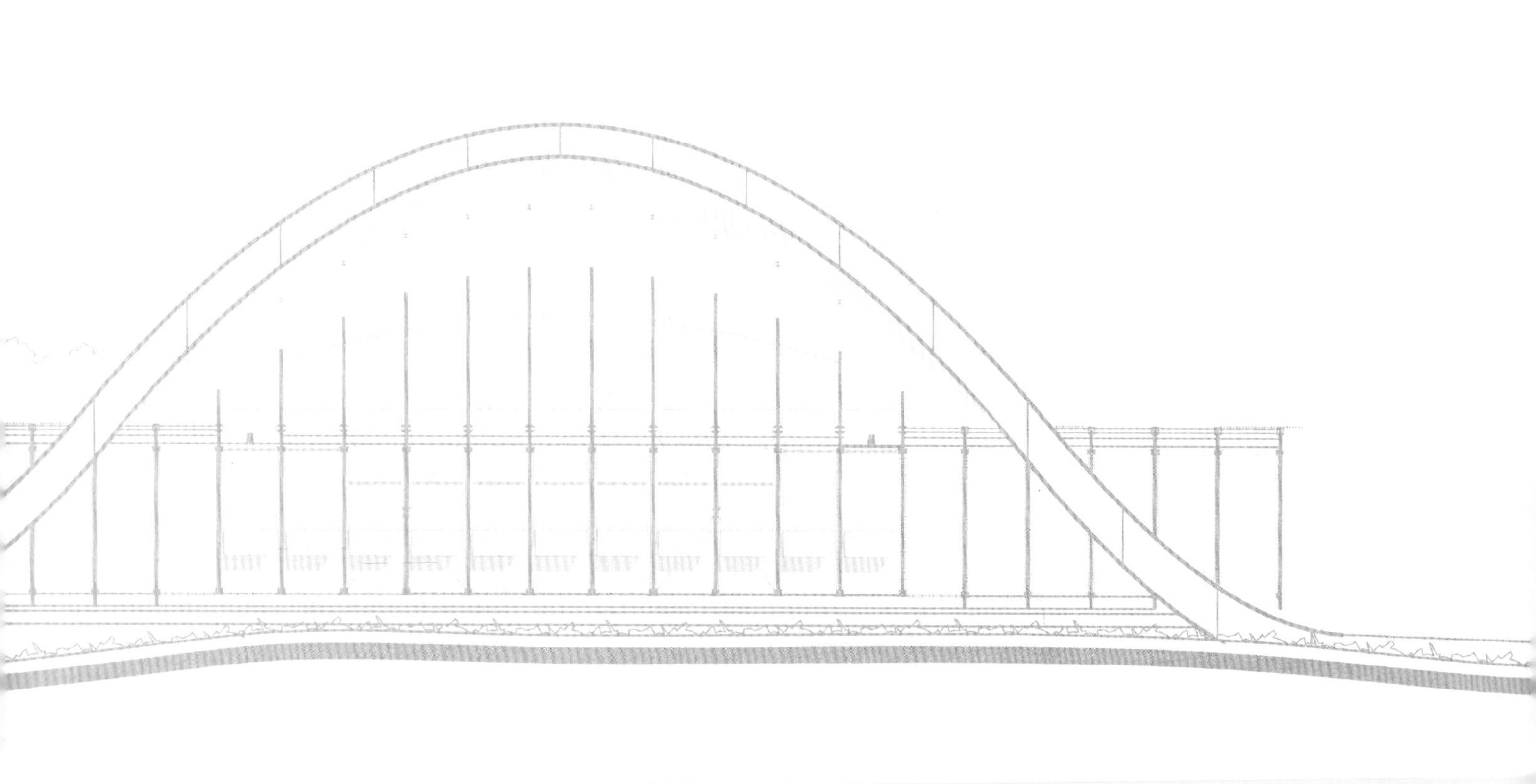

Zentrum Paul Klee, Bern

The Architecture

Contents

From 1998 to 2005, the Maurice E. and Martha Müller Foundation (MMMF) was responsible for the planning, financing, and execution of the building which first opened its doors to the public as the Zentrum Paul Klee, Bern, on June 20, 2005.
Only a few months later, the Zentrum Paul Klee had already firmly established itself as one of Bern's and Switzerland's cultural and tourist attractions, a fact surely due to the exemplary cooperation between private and public sponsors. The Foundation's task was to come up with a building that would create the optimal framework for a museum in which a dialogue could take place between the various artistic disciplines as well as with the public, thus reflecting Paul Klee's own interdisciplinary approach to art.
The realization of this concept was placed in the hands of the architect Renzo Piano and his Building Workshops. In view of the result and of the consistently excellent cooperation with Renzo Piano, his business partner and project coordinator Bernard Plattner, and all the other people involved in the project, this proved to be the right choice. The three hills on the eastern side of the city have become more than just a purpose-built construction. Rather, they are a work of art in their own right, a Landscape Sculpture that presents the artist Paul Klee and his work in just the right light, while making it possible to run a museum that can always find a new direction for that light.

This project replaced the original idea of a monographic Klee museum in Bern. That it could be financed and carried out in such a short time is due entirely to the generosity of private donors: the family of the internationally renowned orthopedic surgeon Professor Maurice E. Müller and his wife Martha Müller-Lüthi, the Lottery Fund of Bern Canton, and the many sponsors from the world of business. We wish to express our deepest thanks to all of them. With their swift and generous commitment they have shown courage and vision and may be assured of public recognition for it.

Peter Schmid
President of the Maurice E. and Martha Müller Foundation, Bern

In the mid-1990s, the City, Canton, and Civic Community of Bern were involved in the planning of a monographic museum dedicated to Paul Klee, based on donations offered by the Klee family. It was to be set up in the historical center of Bern as an annex of the Bern Kunstmuseum. In fact, things turned out quite differently. Thanks to the initiative of Prof. Dr. Maurice E. Müller and his wife Martha Müller-Lüthi, the location of the museum was moved from the town center to the eastern edge of the city, to a district called Schöngrün. The change of paradigm was decided by two aspects of Maurice E. Müller's vision for the center: first of all, he wanted to create something more than just an art museum. In order to do justice to the genius of Paul Klee he felt that what was needed was a cultural center, to make room for Klee's music, theater, literature, and above all his teachings about art. At the same time, the choice of architect was to be made with greatest care: Maurice E. Müller and his family expressed the wish that rather than holding a public competition for the project, the commission should be given directly to a renowned architect. When, in late 1998, the Müller family made public the name of their favored architect, the matter was settled. No one could object to the choice of Renzo Piano and his team to be the architects of the new art and cultural center in Bern.

That choice has turned out to be an entirely fortunate one. Renzo Piano has succeeded admirably in executing the vision of Maurice E. Müller and the ideas of the project directors. In addition, his associate Bernard Plattner—a native of Bern—turned out to be a project director with the skill to combine masterfully his ideas with the requirements of the clients.

If the Zentrum Paul Klee has today become an important destination in Bern, that is not solely due to Paul Klee, but also thanks to the vision of Maurice E. Müller and its realization by Renzo Piano and Bernard Plattner. In just a few months after the opening, the greatest gift Bern has ever received from private persons has become the subject of several thousand pages of international media reports—a remarkable reception. We are proud to be able to present Paul Klee

against the backdrop created by Renzo Piano and Bernard Plattner and, in these three hills, to bring home the full spectrum of his genius to an international public.
It is possible to say on the strength of four months experience that, without a doubt, the architectural and philosophical concept has proven its worth. The building more than meets expectations.

I wish to thank those who helped this book become reality. My thanks go first and foremost to Ursina Barandun, deputy director of the Zentrum Paul Klee. She designed and executed the concept for the opening publications. Special thanks are due to the author, Benedikt Loderer, who followed the construction from its early days. And finally, my heartfelt thanks to Renzo Piano, Bernard Plattner, and Kurt Aellen and their staffs. Working with all of you, dear friends, was a demanding, exciting, and convivial experience of the highest quality.

Andreas Marti
Director of the Zentrum Paul Klee, Bern

Zentrum Paul Klee

Zentrum Paul Klee, Bern

Benedikt Loderer, city wayfarer

The best way to approach the Zentrum Paul Klee is on foot from the west. You alight from bus no. 12 at the second-last stop—Schosshalde—and follow the overhead wires until you arrive at a low rise. The Center is almost opposite. You cannot see the freeway, but its buzz fills the air. Despite the noise of traffic, you have an image of traditional, middle Switzerland before you. On the right there is a village-like group of houses, while a dark line of trees marks the edge of the forest in the background; you have the feeling that the three hills are set in the middle of a huge carpet. They shimmer silver, catching the eye because they don't seem to be part of the familiar picture. They appear small and delicate—from the middle distance their size is hard to comprehend, since there is nothing in the optical memory against which to measure them. Even before you arrive at the site, its ambivalence becomes apparent. You cannot make a final judgment on something so indefinable.

And yet, you know this is it. The Zentrum Paul Klee already belongs to the country's stock of cultural images. Long before you have seen it, the optical equation K = 3W is established in your head. The Klee museum is the one with the three waves.

When you arrive at the bridge over the freeway, the true picture emerges: The carpet drops away, and the noise-reducing walls and a moat full of traffic now dominate the scene. On the wall is a red symbol—the transmutation of a Paul Klee watercolor, Unstable Signpost, painted in 1937. An exclamation mark, originally invented as two-dimensional, now stands there three-dimensional. The observer wonders how it came to be on the wall. You continue past the enormous roofs of what were once farmhouses, and arrive at Villa Schöngrün, freshly renovated and restored as a little jewel case of the petty nobility. You note the word "restaurant" for later.

As you approach the three hills at an acute angle, you see the three waves one after another and gaze in amazement at the flowing double motion: the long, drawn-out, horizontal curve of the hills inclining gently away from us follows the fast-flowing arc of the freeway. This curve connects to the threefold up-and-down of the steel arcs of

Preceding pages: Coming from Schosshalde toward the Zentrum Paul Klee, you see the three hills rising out of the middle of a huge green carpet.

The three hills appear as a natural addition to the Swiss landscape and are set in front of the Gurten, Bern's local mountain.

the hills. The foremost dissolve, some of them curving freely off into the air. The serpentines rest on airy roots, while the green of the surroundings creeps underneath this disciplined tumult. This welcoming view of the center quickly became the photographers' favorite motif.

But before entering the building, it is recommended you take a stroll around the outside. The building? It's really more of a landscape sculpture. "Monument in the Fertile Country" is the motto, drawn from the title of a Klee watercolor. The path takes you in a wide curve to a rise, and you can no longer see a building. It now looks like three strange artificial bumps growing up out of a field—or more precisely, that are part of the field. It is not a house, a building, or even a structure: it is a part of the landscape that has been shaped and domesticated.

The walk is calming and slows you down. You look beyond the three silvery hills to the Gurten, the local mountain, and think you can discern the city spread out in the foreground behind the wavy horizon. A farmer drives by on his tractor, and the atmosphere is bucolic. A detour to the Sculpture Park, created by the Zurich landscape architects Eduard Neuenschwander and Anja Bandorf in conjunction with the Renzo Piano Building Workshop, provides a quiet perspective from which to grasp the project. Here, in strange isolation on meandering gravel paths, flanked by the sculptures of Oscar Wiggli, Alicia Penalba, and Yves Dana and with the birch avenues vis-à-vis, one senses the dimension of quiet that is an essential part of the Zentrum Paul Klee. As is the noise of the freeway. But you have to take in both to grasp the whole. Quiet and the rush of traffic are not mutually exclusive—they are ambivalently linked.

Homo Faber

The Sculpture Park is also the best place to do your homework. Piano? Who is Renzo Piano, and how does he come to be here, in the fertile country?

The Zentrum Paul Klee is the fourth museum built by Renzo Piano. Its forerunners are the Centre Pompidou, the Menil Collection, and the Fondation Beyeler. You have to keep these projects in mind when considering the building in Bern, because Piano learns something on each project that will be useful for the next.

But first—who is Renzo Piano? Le Corbusier stressed at every opportunity that his family was descended from the Cathars, and that was why he was so rebellious and inflexible. Renzo Piano likewise never misses a chance to tell people that he is the son of a master builder,

Renzo Piano the architect is the son and grandson of architects. He always begins with the concrete task at hand, never with abstract theory.

and that his grandfather was also a master builder, all of which gave him a love of making things. "I used to go to building sites with my father when I was little, I was fascinated by seeing how things were created from nothing by the hand of man alone. To a child, a building site is a magical place: one day, you see a pile of bricks and sand; the next day, it has become a wall; and finally, a whole building stands there, big and solid, and people live in it. I have had the great fortune to be able to spend my life doing what I dreamed of as a child."[1]

For Piano it's obvious: with this paternal background, no other career was possible. Of course he became an architect. In conversation, he names Brunelleschi as one of his idols. From time to time, he compares himself with Robinson Crusoe, a man who knew how to survive on unknown terrain using his practical intelligence. The architecture critic Kenneth Frampton summed it up thus: "Throughout his career, Piano has worked towards a myth-free architecture, with one exception: the myth of the inborn, world-creating primeval urge of a Homo Faber."[2]

Born in Genoa in 1937, Piano studied architecture in Florence and Milan. Ernesto Rogers and Giancarlo De Carlo were his most important teachers and role models. He calls Richard Buckminster Fuller and Pier Luigi Nervi, his "distant teachers" and feels close to the ideas of Jean Prouvé, to his "special manner of carrying out this profession."[3] Prouvé, it should be mentioned, has Bern connections: he was a consultant on earlier projects by the ARB office, which, as Piano's representative in Bern, coordinated and supervised the construction of the Zentrum Paul Klee.

After completing his diploma at Milan Polytechnic in 1964, Piano began to experiment. He worked with tension and pressure and built big things out of nothing. He developed light constructions out of rods, cables, and membranes, introduced shells made out of the new material polyester into his buildings, and put together spatial structures out of prefabricated pieces. The Robinson Crusoe of the 1960s was an explorer, who used the most modern technology and materials without hesitation. Then, as now, his goal is lightness. The constructions themselves must be light, but so must the serious game of discovering them. Renzo Piano is never "heavy-handed." When Robinson Crusoe and Homo Faber get together, they never look for a style; they search for solutions.

As someone who believes architecture is for people, Piano has always made himself accessible to the public. He used a television series, for example, to tell the public what he had learned about lightweight construction. Architecture for architects has never interested him.

The energy conveyor for consumers of culture: The Centre Pompidou in Paris was the most influential building of the 1970s.

The culture machine, opened in 1977, was acclaimed by the public, mistrustfully admired by architects.

The Culture Machine

In the public mind, Piano's name is linked with the Centre Pompidou in Paris. Together with his then-partner Richard Rogers, Piano won the international competition for the project ahead of 680 other entrants. This success established Piano on the world stage. Ever since then, he has been one of the world's best known architects for major projects.

"I was 33 at the time, I was a wild boy. Richard, too—we were the Beatles. It was a rebellion against museums."[4] Piano and Rogers, assisted by the engineer Peter Rice of Ove Arup & Partners, decided to go for broke and designed a radically different kind of museum. They turned the glove inside-out, making the inside the outside. Inside are the wide spaces without supports, outside are the installations and the utilities connections, mounted on the exterior of the façade.

When the Centre Pompidou was completed in 1977, it became the architectural sensation of the decade—celebrated by the public and admired mistrustfully by architects. It was more than just a building, it was a culture machine. Its cascade of escalators caught the imagination and became the center's logo. This culture machine may be what Le Corbusier was thinking of when he spoke of a "machine à émouvoir." The Centre Pompidou still impresses today with its immense presence. It is surrounded by three squares like a modern cathedral, an integral part of central Paris. Terrible beauté!

It was Piano's first museum, although it is not actually a museum but a energy conveyor for consumers of culture. On an average day, 25,000 visitors stream through its escalator tubes; more than 180 million people have visited it to date. The building is as important to them as the exhibitions. The Centre Pompidou is just as much an automatic stop on the tourist itinerary as Nôtre Dame, and it has the same number of stars as Nôtre Dame in the travel guide. One enters the building and enjoys the view of the city, hardly noticing that everything that people find exciting happens on the façades, the roof, and on the plazas outside—but not really inside. The breathtaking trip to the top, the galleries outside the halls, the viewing platforms, and the fire-eaters on the square in front of the building.

Only when you look closer you see what the Centre Pompidou really is—a huge stack of artificially-lit spaces, a multi-purpose hall distributed over six floors. There is no architecture left inside, the rooms are black boxes, nothing more than vessels for ever-changing fixtures. The Centre Pompidou is an exterior building. Everything that makes it interesting is on its façades. One need only compare the

The Menil Collection in Houston, Texas, stands as a gray-white art coffer in suburbia.

The Light Machine: Piano developed an ingenious system of repeating modular elements.

There is an atmosphere of dignified reason. Madame de Menil invites you to her salon.

Centre Pompidou with the new Staatsgalerie in Stuttgart—built seven years later in 1984 by James Stirling, with traditional halls lit from above—to see what the Centre Pompidou, for all its cleverness, is missing—light.

The Light Machine

"Houston is a city with no memory, Paris a city with too much,"[5] Piano once said in an interview. Thus, his second museum had to be quite different from his first. In his building for the Menil Collection in Houston, Texas, which opened in 1986, light is the main architectural theme.

The story might have come straight out of a cheap novel: an oil magnate dies and leaves behind a fortune, an art collection, and a widow who is a scion of wealthy French aristocrats. She decides to spend the money to build a museum as a fitting home for the collection. The Menil Collection is in all things the opposite of the Centre Pompidou. It is located in US suburbia, not in the center of Paris. Amid loosely scattered suburban homes stands a low, gray-white art coffer. An entire block between four streets has been left free of houses, forming a meadow in which the museum is set.

This is not about teaching and entertaining crowds of tourists; this is a place of contemplation. The museum is simply structured. A large, single-story rectangle holds the rooms in which the temporary exhibitions take place. Piano set a narrow bar along one long side of the flat roof. This contains offices and the treasury of some 10,000 art objects.

Piano is a modern architect, a functionalist of the inventive kind. He has spent a long time thinking about the relationship between art and technology. He is engaged in a "personal war of liberation against the mythology of 'creation.'" He believes that "the artist is not blessed with a 'gift,' rather he masters a technique and understands how to make use of it to achieve his goal: art."[6] The Menil Collection is a concrete example of this belief.

Light is natural light, otherwise it is not light. Here it comes from above, from the zenith. As a response to this idea, Piano developed the dominant element of the museum—the transparent roof. The ground plan and the internal organization of the museum are clever and practical, there is an atmosphere of dignified reason, which treats the museum as a traditional temple of the religion of art. Madame de Menil invites you into her salon.

But Piano wants more than a cultivated ambience. He aims to control the mood, and for that he must control the light. He has invented

Four parallel wall panels support the delicate roof of the Fondation Beyeler, which opened in 1997.

The light roof perches upon the walls like a butterfly.

The most significant thing is invisible. The technical requirements for the lighting are hidden in the ceiling.

a clever system of roof elements which work in concert. The so-called "light leaves," organically shaped concrete louvers, are the result of a step-by-step approach. Fixed to a steel framework, they filter and distribute the light, reduce the volume of light, afford protection from the sun, and form the wave pattern on the ceiling of the exhibition rooms.

In finding a solution to the problem of natural light, Piano also finds a solution to the main problem—the museum.

Piano did not resort to the traditional solution of building a glass roof with a dust sheet under it—such as we know from the museums of the nineteenth century, and which was employed by Stirling in Stuttgart, by Gigon Guyer for the Kirchner Museum in Davos, and by Morger Degelo for the Liechtenstein Kunstmuseum Vaduz. Piano does not go about a project with preconceived ideas. Conventional ideas obscure the view of better ones. He does not accept pre-formulated solutions. He works prototypically, carefully, makes assumptions, tests their consequences, changes them, works in variations, approaches the solution by circling around it. He does not reject anything more emphatically than the myth of the architectural genius, in whose brains, blood, and balls inspiration comes like a flash of lightening from above.

The Wall

Ernst Beyeler saw the Menil Collection and was convinced that Piano was the right architect for his museum. At the Fondation Beyeler in Riehen, outside Basel, Piano sank the building into the ground, making a large volume almost disappear within the park.

Piano, the master builder, keeps both feet firmly on the ground. He says there is no general solution—the important thing is always the location. "I believe this project is the best proof that we are fundamentally regionalists, so tied to a place that we stay where we are, that we never move away."[7] Everything begins with a reading of the location: "We stand there and we say, aha, so this is what it looks like here."[8] Piano found a narrow, slightly undulating piece of vineyard bordered by a wall. The wall separates the road from the land—that is what it was built for. But a wall does more than that. It directs the view, creating an in-front-of and a behind. It turns its back on the road and looks out at the landscape, sees an open field in front of it, beyond that a plain, and on the horizon Tüllinger hill, its crown adorned with something medieval. A picture postcard.

The wall is old, it tells a story—of a patrician manor, of a ruler, of bygone forms of agriculture and production. The wall tells of privileges

and how they crumble away. (The Schöngrün manor tells a similar story.) Walls are built to protect, to exclude, to shut in.
This wall must have made a deep impression on Piano, for he turned it into a generative element in his design. He constructed a museum from a series of four parallel walls. They reach into the park and anchor the building in the ground. They establish the horizontal and cut through the waveforms of the ground, which only serves to emphasize the shape of the land.
The walls are heavy. Piano, a maker of lightweight buildings, took particular pleasure in giving weight to these walls. He gave them a cladding of red Patagonian porphyry. This stone, he explained, is geologically ancient, created even before the continents drifted apart. Will one day the mere fragments of the four parallel walls of the Fondation Beyeler remain to bear witness to what once was? Piano says he never thought of the ruins of the future. Whether he did or not, these walls are the opposite of his first works. Nothing here is light or transient.
Except for one thing—the roof. Piano celebrates the contrast of the heavy walls with the light roof, which perches upon the walls like a butterfly alighting. Yet the link between the roof and the walls remains hidden—nowhere is the construction visible from the outside. Here, the technical demands are greater—ecology being a keyword—and yet, it is as if the urge to demonstrate how the whole thing is put together—as in the Centre Pompidou—has been blown away. Piano no longer has to prove anything.
"I do not see why we [...] should not have employed every possible technique we have learned to date in ways of using light, in the preservation and conservation of works of art, and the use of glass."[9]
In taking the step from the Menil Collection to the Fondation Beyeler Piano went through an important learning experience. Rebellion is no longer an architectural theme—now he is very civilized. Showing off the workings of the building has given way to a mastery of light. It is also the transition from heliography to computer printout. Put another way: Piano has learned to use a computer as a design and drafting instrument. And he does so masterfully.

The Design Machine

Piano has thought long and hard about the business of being an architect. "It is a borderline profession, hovering between art and science, walking the tightrope between invention and memory, between the courage of the modern and respect for tradition."[10]
He compares designers with explorers: Columbus, Magellan, Cook,

The Renzo Piano Building Workshop is always a hum with thought and experimentation.

Calculate and work. Trial and error. The design process oscillates between tinkering and totaling.

Amundsen. The architect goes on a voyage of discovery, and designing is an adventure.

That means it is beset with dangers: "Incompetence, lack of responsibility, presumptuousness, and a contempt for the craft are the things that demean our profession and destroy it."[11] He opposes "line of least resistance" architecture, as promised by clever salesmen, and is equally sharp in his rejection of those who live in ivory towers—they "take pleasure in their real or imagined ineffectuality in society. It is a classic standpoint taken to wriggle out of any responsibility and to serve as an excuse to flee into pure form or into technology."[12] When he received the Pritzker Prize in 1998—the Nobel Prize of architecture—he said in his acceptance speech: "Therefore I see in [architecture] above all the curiosity, the social expectations, the thirst for adventure: these are the motives that have kept me out of the temple."[13]

For Piano, the opposite of the academic temple is the practical workplace. He calls it the Renzo Piano Building Workshop (RPBW)—a place to think and experiment. There are two: one in Genoa with some forty lively, thinking people, and one in Paris with around fifty. The Paris workshop, which helped plan the Zentrum Paul Klee, is situated in the center of town on Rue des Archives 34. Its display window affords passersby a view directly into the model-building workshop—a typical Piano gesture. Models—in fact, handcrafting of all kinds—are a vital part of Renzo Piano's design methods. Architects rely on seeing and feeling. They have to touch what they see, and they have to make visible what they visualize. The Building Workshop is a buzzing hive, stuffed full of models, presentations, books, and computers.

Calculate and work. Trial and error, first on paper, then as a model, then eventually as a prototype on a scale of one to one, that is the method of the practical scientist Renzo Piano and his people. The design process oscillates between tinkering and totaling, the simplest hand-drawn sketches and the most hi-tech computer drawings are used. It is a fascinating mixture of playfulness and calculated precision. On the way there are detours, roundabout routes, dead ends to be got out of, but every step is one step closer to an as yet undefined goal. The detours are necessary—they ensure that no short circuits, no apparent short cuts, lead to a rash, ill-considered result. Anyone who commits himself too soon locks himself in. Piano's people approach their task like a team of researchers on thin ice. The model is not there to impress the client, it is an instrument of discovery. The working process must always be illustrated. Every step is documented and becomes a part of the growing exhibition—which is also there to provide information for those working within the organization. People here speak in images. Those working here come from all over the world, and most of them are young; they all learn the visual language of the Building Workshop. Piano speaks in striking images. "We can only realize one project if we are simultaneously working on five others,"[14] says Bernard Plattner, project director of the Zentrum Paul Klee. At any given time, they are working on several projects at once, and anyone working on one hears all about the others as well. A workshop means talking about the work as well as doing it.

The Building Workshop is an intellectual powerhouse. Piano sums it up thus: "In architecture, everything mixes and everything contradicts. But contradictions are the salt of life. Take the opposites of art and science. For me, they are two dimensions which are not mutually exclusive, rather, they exist parallel to each other. Architecture is both an art and a science. Without science, you can't make art, that is clear. We have quite a lot of experience of that in our team. We have so much knowledge that we are sometimes able to forget about it, like a good pianist who no longer has to think about his technique and loses himself in his playing."[15]

Paul Klee in his Bauhaus studio, Weimar, 1922

Ephrosina Grezhova, Felix and Paul Klee, Basel, fall 1931

The Road to the Klee Museum

When Renzo Piano was born in 1937, Paul Klee had only three years to live. He died on June 29, 1940, in Locarno, leaving some 6,000 works to his wife, Lily Klee. Their only child, Felix, was working as a theater director in Germany at the time. In a contract with his mother, he renounced his claim to part of the estate and in return received financial assistance from his mother. Despite his weak eyesight, he was drafted into the German army toward the end of World War II and sent to Poland. He became a prisoner of war under the Russians in January 1945 and was believed dead. But in mid-September 1946, he returned to his wife, Ephrosina Klee-Grezhova, and their only child, Alexander, born in 1940.

The war was over, and German assets in Switzerland were frozen. Because Paul Klee died before receiving Swiss citizenship, his wife and son were still German citizens. This had serious consequences. After the death of Lily Klee on September 22, 1946, there was a danger that the estate of Paul Klee would be broken up. The Washington Accord of 1946 between Switzerland and the Allies meant the assets of Germans living in Switzerland were to be liquidated and the funds used for reparation.

Lily Klee, probably Lucerne, summer 1946

Livia Klee-Meyer and Felix Klee in the park of the Louisiana Museum, Humlebæk, 1986

Signing of the foundation deed of the Stiftung Paul Klee-Zentrum, September 15, 2000; from right to left: Alexander Klee, President of the Paul-Klee-Stiftung, Bernhard Hahnloser, Vice President of the Paul-Klee-Stiftung, Dr. Hans Lauri, Councilor of the Canton of Bern, Dr. Klaus Baumgartner, Mayor and Representative of the City of Bern

Lily Klee gave power of attorney to Rolf Bürgi, an insurance agent, and he became the driving force behind the foundation of the Klee-Gesellschaft (Klee Society), which purchased the estate—thereby preventing its seizure. In 1947, the Klee-Gesellschaft became the Paul-Klee-Stiftung, which at the time considered building a Klee Museum. Ultimately, however, it chose to integrate the Klee estate into the Kunstmuseum Bern. The true heir, Felix Klee, launched a legal action, which in 1952 resulted in the transferal of title to him of well over a thousand works. But as president of the Paul-Klee-Stiftung, he ensured that the two parts of the collection remained united.

Felix Klee died in August 1990. His son Alexander took the decisive step toward the foundation of a Klee museum in 1993, when he committed himself to keeping the family collection together on condition that a museum be built in Bern. Then it was the turn of his stepmother, Livia Klee-Meyer, whom Felix had married in 1980 after the death of his first wife. Livia, daughter of the architect and Bauhaus director Hannes Meyer, donated the works allocated to her to the Canton and the City of Bern in the early summer of 1997. In November 1998, Alexander Klee signed a permanent loan contract for the future Klee museum. That meant the unification of the works held by the Paul-Klee-Stiftung, the Livia Klee Donation, and the works on permanent loan from Alexander—all in all, more than 40 percent of Paul Klee's artistic output. Livia Klee-Meyer was generous, but she was also clear in her aims. If the museum was not open by December 31, 2006—she stipulated—her donation would become null and void. She was determined to beat the notoriously slow pace of operations in Bern.

Soon after Alexander's first proposals, a working group of museum people and culture officials was charged with the task of finding a location for the museum. They quickly settled on the former schoolhouse on Waisenhausplatz. They were ambitious, planning a museum of contemporary art next to the Klee museum, both of which would be linked with the nearby Kunstmuseum Bern. They dreamed of a Museum Island in the heart of Bern.

How Klee and Piano Came Together

But there was opposition to this scheme, above all from the architects, who felt the schoolhouse was too musty and wanted a new building. A study commissioned by the project directors found a suitable site at the head of the Lorraine bridge, very close to the Kunstmuseum. This plan for a new building looked set to go ahead, and an international architectural competition had been proposed for 1999, when one man—the surgeon Prof. Dr. Maurice E. Müller—suddenly changed

Professor Maurice E. Müller, the architect Renzo Piano, and Martha Müller-Lüthi in front of the Zentrum Paul Klee, 2004

all the rules of the game. In July 1998, the astonished people of Bern were told that the world-famous inventor of the artificial hip would donate 30 million Swiss francs to the Klee museum, would also donate the land, and had already chosen the architect: Renzo Piano. Müller had met him through the pianist Maurizio Pollini, whom the surgeon had successfully operated on in the wake of a serious accident. Piano and Pollini have been friends since their youth.

But Müller wanted more than just a Klee museum: it was to be a cultural center, in which music, literature, theater, and dance could take their place alongside Klee and the visual arts. Müller also wanted it to include a children's museum and conference facilities.

Bern was amazed—that kind of patronage was unheard of in this city. Delight was mixed with skepticism. Schöngrün was at the edge of town, the idea of a museum of contemporary art would be torn out of context, and the competition—which the younger architects had fought for and hoped to win—would simply not happen. And yet it soon became clear that Bern could not afford to turn down Müller's gift. One look at the city's finances was enough to dampen the heated arguments, and there was little hope that an expensive culture project would be backed by the necessary referendum. So all those involved quickly decided to get things moving. In November 1998, the Canton of Bern, the City of Bern, and the Civic Community of Bern signed a contract with Maurice E. Müller and his wife Martha Müller-Lüthi, outlining the division of labor: the Maurice E. and Martha Müller Foundation (MMMF)—specially founded for the purpose—was to be responsible for the building, and the public authorities would become the future operators of the Zentrum Paul Klee (ZPK).

In December 1999, the results of a year's planning by Renzo Piano and his Building Workshop were revealed to the public. Piano presented his ideas for the project in an exhibition at the Kornhaus—Bern's showcase for architecture and design—and in a special edition of the architecture magazine Hochparterre. With the exception of the concert hall, which was a later addition, the plans were executed as Piano set them out then, with a few necessary adjustments.

At the new location the expectations were no less than at the old site. Bern aimed to become an international city of culture. The then-Canton Councilor Hans Lauri declared: "The involvement of the Müller family offers the City, the Canton, and the Civic Community of Bern a unique opportunity to create a center for art whose radiance will extend beyond the borders of the canton and the country."[16]

But there were still political hurdles to be taken. The Canton Parliament backed the proposal in November 2000 with an overwhelming majority. The Bern City Council gave it the nod three days later with a vote of sixty-six in favor to none against. And a referendum in the city of Bern in March 2001 also yielded a clear result—78 percent of Bern citizens were in favor of the project. The initial skepticism had evaporated, and the objections of architects and the culture lobby were no longer an issue.

It all happened at a pace uncharacteristic of Bern. The building permit was issued in October 2001, the foundation stone laid in June 2002, the topping-out ceremony was in December 2003, and on June 20, 2005, even before the official opening, members of the public were able to enter the Zentrum Paul Klee for the first time. Instead of a museum island in the center of town, they now had a building standing alone in the countryside. The administration and events held there also took place alone, as the close cooperation with the Kunstmuseum and the Kunsthalle that the Zentrum Paul Klee had hoped for did not (initially at least) come about.

The Hill

Prof. Dr. Maurice E. Müller had seen the Fondation Beyeler in Riehen near Basel—and that convinced him of Piano's talent. Müller probably envisaged a museum similar to the Basel Museum, and indeed, the land seemed suitable for this kind of a building. But Piano reacted as Piano does. As they stood at the site for the first time, Maurice E. Müller, Renzo Piano, and Bernard Plattner, the project director, all realized that they could not accommodate Klee in any "normal building." They agreed that one needs time and space for Klee—and then there was this hill, which they took photographs of straight away. It was not very high, but it was a very attractive hill. And of course, they took in the full effect of the freeway, which cut through the landscape. In this semi-rural setting, the noise of the freeway made it obvious where they were: amid the agglomeration of Bern at the end of the twentieth century.

What Piano saw, experienced, and felt in 1998 he summarized shortly thereafter in a letter to Maurice E. Müller: "Where to begin? With Paul Klee, of course. It is the dimension of calm which best suits this artist. A poet of calm ought to make one think about a museum of a fundamentally quiet nature."[17] Piano listened to the sounds within, and there he heard Klee the musician.

The design began with a thorough exploration of Paul Klee and of the site. The freeway is not a necessary evil to be repressed—rather, it is a vital artery for the city. The project had to be developed with the freeway, not against it. Precise observations of the rise and fall of

Piano saw not a high, but a particularly beautiful hill on his first visit to the site. The hill became the central idea of this project.

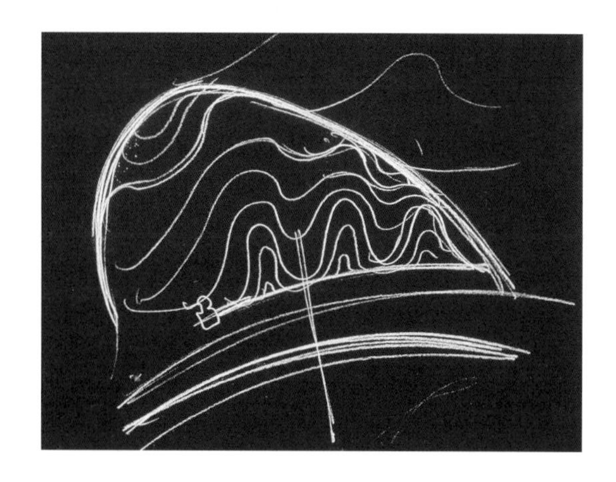

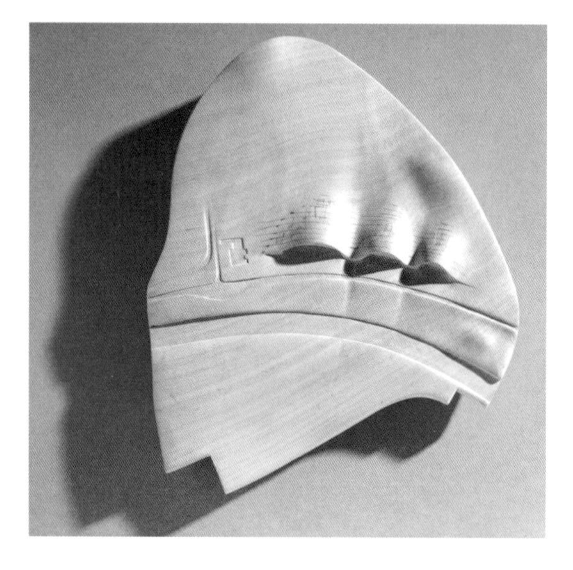

The idea of the Landscape Sculpture with the three hills arose in an early freehand sketch.

The grooves scratched on the wooden model represent early ideas about the visible steel ribs.

the land led to the first sketches. Klee's grave at the nearby Schosshalden cemetery was a discovery. "I am not at all unhappy that the work of this artist [...] will be kept for ever at a place of inner composure, not far from the cemetery where he rests. But that is only possible far from the noise of the city. To achieve this, the site must be large. I think the work you are asking of me will have to take in the whole property, from the buildings in the east to the freeway in the west," he wrote in the letter.[18]

Schöngrün was a fine piece of land, zoned for building, behind the freeway and not far from Freudenbergerplatz. Maurice E. Müller, who himself lives at the edge of the site, had in 1982 set the ball rolling with a two-phase private competition for the site's future buildings. The lion's share of the property was subsequently built on, but one part remained empty. Müller originally proposed to put a residential and cultural center on the block, but this plan was never realized. A piece of land was looking for a new function. Müller decided to donate it to the public for a Klee museum.

However, Piano quickly convinced all those concerned that the land originally intended for the museum was not appropriate. He suggested building the new museum in an empty field reserved for the expansion of the cemetery. Piano explained it thus: "We mustn't make it small; the whole thing has to be integrated into the planning. As soon as we had decided to work on the basis of the entirety, the matter was no longer one of just a building—it was about a place. And so, from then on, we regarded the site as a sculpture and worked the field like farmers."[19] That land belonged to the City of Bern and was in the agricultural zone. Hence, this new demand was far beyond the legal building limitations and Müller's offer, and yet it created the foundation for the core idea of the design, the hill. "As I have already told you, I find the genius loci of this place in the gentle undulation of the hill,"[20] Piano wrote to Müller. The hill in Schöngrün is the spiritual brother of the wall in Riehen. Ultimately it became three hills. The waveform of the three hills is Piano's arbitrary invention. The hills did not arise from the need to build a museum. They came from the reading of the location—not from any architectural philosophy. Being an architect also entails convincing people. That Piano was able to convince Maurice E. Müller and the City and Canton of Bern to agree to this change is among the architect's most important achievements on the whole project. That's something only Piano can do. It is clear that Renzo Piano wanted to build these hills. He alone. He found them, he invented them, he convinced everyone, and now—one has to admit—they are magnificent.

Castrum Lunatum

Where there are no hills, one must make them. Piano constructed a building and created a landscape around it. The artifact and domesticated nature hold each other in balance. The hills are two things at the same time: they are art buildings, in the literal sense, and they are also the articulation of a landscape. They are the museum's own trademark, which engraves itself on the memory. The graphic abbreviation of the threefold wave became the logo of the Zentrum Paul Klee, just as the escalators became that of the Centre Pompidou. Seen from the freeway, the three curves of the roof appear for ten seconds—an unexpected shape heralding something out of the ordinary. Their message is: this place is important, there must be something valuable behind it. The words written on the wall confirm that: Zentrum Paul Klee. Seen from the park, the three mysterious waves give the observer a feeling of uncertainty. What is being camouflaged here? Piano believes in a secret link between imagination

The terrain was depicted—or rather, explored—using models. The building is not a house, but is understood as part of the landscape.

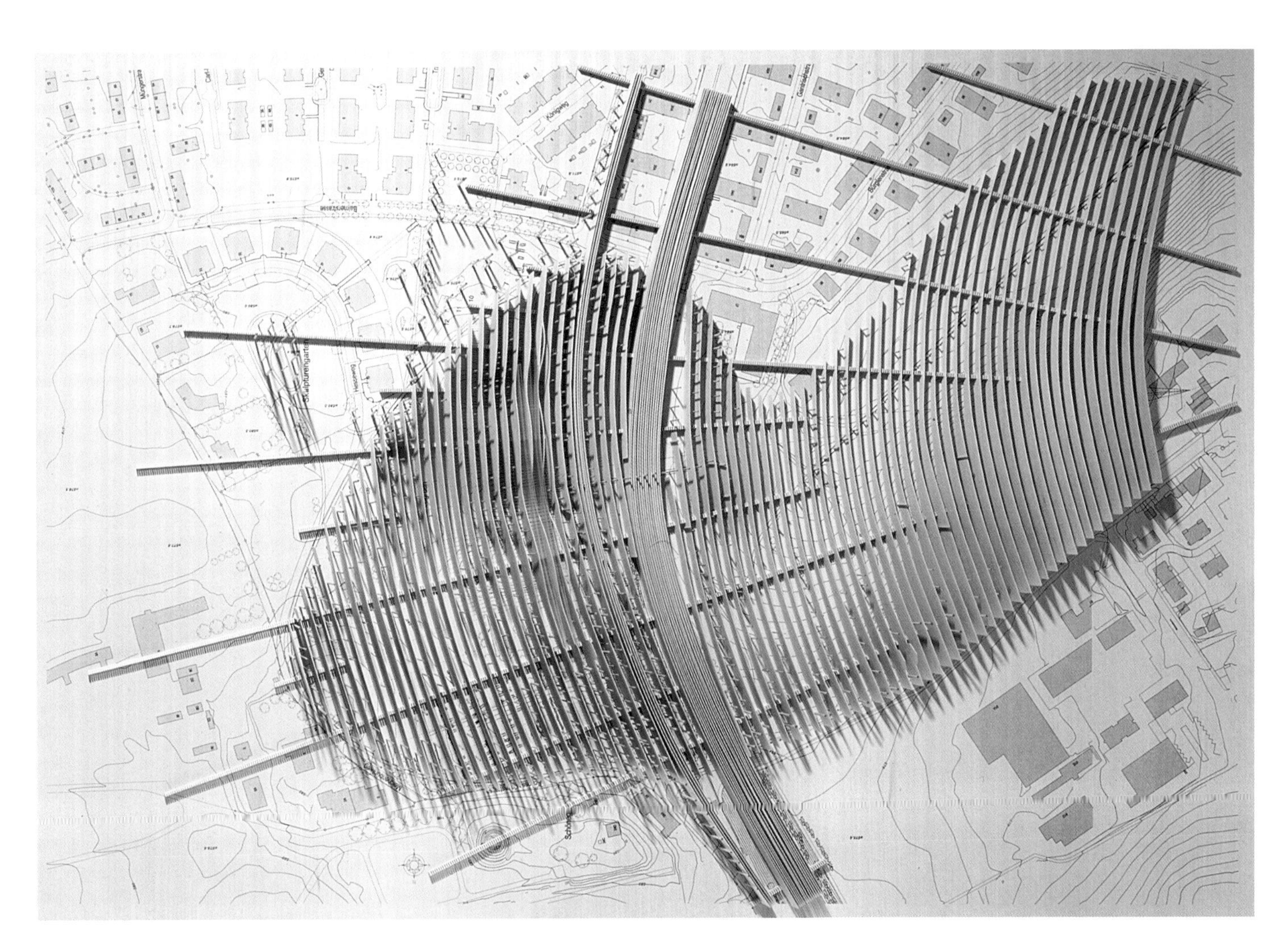

The city of Bern extends from the old town to the Alps. In the middle, on the meandering line of the freeway, is the future building site.

and landscape; it creates the aura of naturalness in the artificial. Looking at the model, one is reminded of a crescent-shaped fortress, a sunken castrum lunatum,[21] set in a shelf of land which follows the long curve of an old city wall. Piano outlined the wall once more with an enormous steel profile. The freeway is the moat, the inclined façade the remains of a fortress. Only a small part of the bulk of the building shows above the surface—what remains is below the surface, and what was once a fortress has been taken away by time.
A different image: the ribs of the roof supports descend into the ground, giving the impression that something has risen to the surface. An unknown, technological beast has pushed its way up out of the earth to draw breath. And yet another image: this is how the landscape looked as left behind by the melting of the Aare glacier at the end of the last ice age. Three hard monadnocks sit close together, smoothed round by the ice and scraped clean. Humans flattened them down over time, and Piano has now artificially restored the natural form.
"We are building a home for Paul Klee, but a building is a building and not a work by Paul Klee,"[22] Piano reminds us. Architecture is not a mere handmaid of art, and Piano does not see himself as a service provider whose work should be as invisible as possible. "It is nonsense to suggest that a museum should be completely neutral. And it is equally absurd if the museum as a work of art smothers its contents."[23] Piano places himself next to Klee, not below him. "I have to look at Klee's work so as to forget it and do my own work."[24] The work of art remains autonomous, regardless of whether it is by a painter or an architect. The two may be related, but they are not of the same family.

The Agglomeration Exists

Where is Schöngrün? In the middle of the edge of the city. The choice of Schöngrün raised many eyebrows. People in Bern say the city runs from the Heiliggeistkirche to the Nydegg Bridge; anything outside the curve of the Aare is no longer Bern but the outskirts. Schöngrün is even further out, considered by many to be in the countryside. Piano admired Bern's historical center, but he did not know where the city's boundaries lay. He saw the context of the landscape and not the hierarchy of city districts. He contrasted the compact old town with the open spaces of Schöngrün and their natural extension through Wyssloch to the Egelsee lake, including the forested summit of the Ostermundigenberg. With the discovery of Schöngrün the Bernese gained a new perspective on their home town. Suddenly,

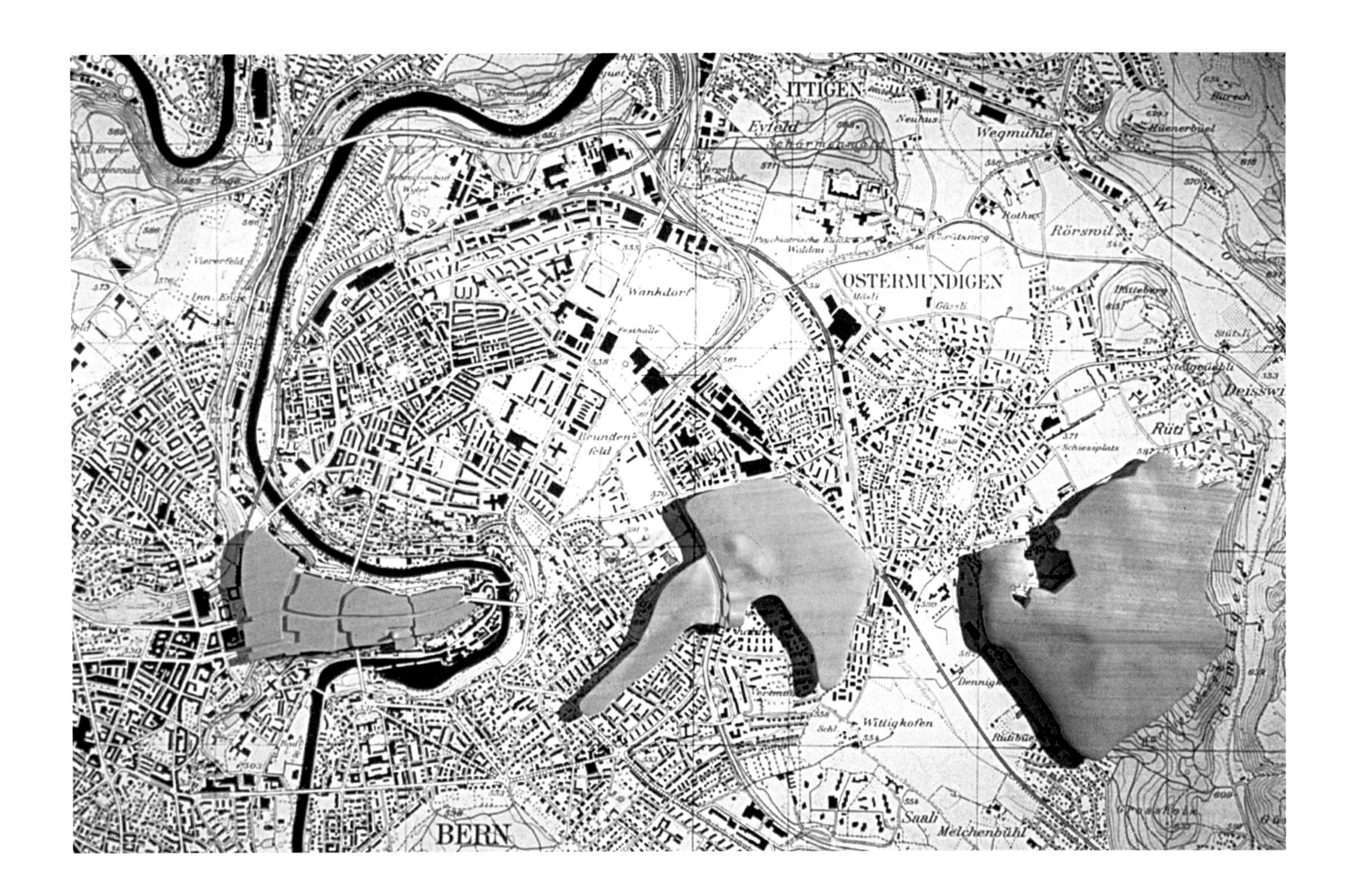

Renzo Piano contrasts the open areas of Egelsee lake (and its continuation into Wyssloch), Schöngrün, and Ostermundigenberg with the heavily built-up old town.

Bern was bigger than its inhabitants believed it to be. It finally made sense to accept the urban sprawl as a modern reality, instead of focusing solely on the old town. The battle for a Bern museum island in the historic heart of the city was dominated by this fixation, and Schöngrün is perhaps the first step toward a realistic view of matters as they stand—the agglomeration of Bern exists.

Schöngrün. The name of the district means "lovely green" in German and says it all. Anyone who strolls along the path bordering the three hills of the Zentrum Paul Klee will be surrounded by a calming green environment. Like many painters and landscape designers before him, Renzo Piano employed the classic technique of using levels to make a structure. In the foreground are the three "hills" of the museum. Beyond them is the middle ground of trees and gardens and on the edge of the forest. These merge into the background of the surrounding wooded hills. The eye is guided in such a way that it does not perceive the agglomeration of the city of Bern. One feels the woods reach as far as the horizon. Near and far meld into one another, and the green of the complex grounds appears like an island

in a sea of trees. On a clear day, you can even see the Alps and the three holy peaks of the Bernerland: the Eiger, the Mönch, and the Jungfrau. Piano has created a place secret and transported in its isolation. Yet the background of noise from the freeway reminds us that we are in the midst of the agglomeration.

Metamorphosis

Now you have done your homework, your walk is over, and you arrive back where you started. Now, to get inside. But the entrance is not where you expect it to be. It is not at the northern end of Museum Street, nor is it in the axis of the first hill. The path takes a tricky turn and leads you in an arc past the glass membrane of North Hill. You see some children behind the façade, working away at a long table.

Put another way: the Kindermuseum Creaviva is the first thing the visitor sees—and that underlines the message that communication is the primary task of the Zentrum Paul Klee. The path arrives at the first valley, where a curved bridge crosses the moat and reaches the glass canal of Museum Street.

But even before one enters the building, Piano reveals what he means by the word metamorphosis. You arrive vertically in the glass canal and there are two ways you can look: you can turn to the left or the right along Museum Street, or your attention is drawn straight ahead. You see the gently inclined depression between the hills, and the slopes of the hills rising to the left and right. Your gaze travels on to the edge of the forest and the Ostermundigenberg behind it. Metamorphosis here means the melding and merging of the artificial,

The model of the site contours became the memento to those who made the Zentrum Paul Klee possible.

Upon arrival, you can see right through. The entrance is situated in a valley, allowing the landscape to shine through.

grassy landscape with the metal skin of the roof. A zone of gratings and metal tubs filled with earth, in which the grass grows and which are suspended between the ribs of the building, mediates between the grass-grown valley and the metal slopes. The ribs of the chrome-plated girders bury themselves in the grass or seem to grow out of it. "The contours are disguised in the finest camouflage manner. After some initial irritation, it seems only logical that the roof shines at the front and leaves freestanding girders behind."[25] Barely have you entered the building, before your attention is captured by the outside of the valley and the transition. Piano aims to confuse. That is why he placed the entrance in the valley between the first two hills.

Museum Street

Museum Street is the most successful space in the Zentrum Paul Klee. It has that cheerful self-assurance typical of all Piano's best buildings—and yet it still surprises. It makes the threefold wave accessible from inside; the high-ceilinged foyers in the hills are linked by relatively low glass corridors. This creates a series of spaces, alternately broad and narrow. This is underlined by the modern enfilade—one's gaze runs along the entire length of Museum Street, and you feel the curve of the freeway, the arc which sets the tone of the entire ground plan.

Museum Street is the backbone of the complex. It provides a view through this modern enfilade. You perceive the arc which is the starting point for the entire ground plan.

The corridors are in fact bridges across the building's valleys, balconies from which to view the backs of the hills on the one side and the landscape on the other. One never has the feeling one is walking along a corridor. Wherever you look outside, you never feel confined. One of the steel arches lowers itself toward Museum Street, perforates the floor, and reappears on the other side of the valley. The arch is wrapped in a metal skin, and one can see the metalwork up close. Each one of these metal plates, perfectly welded together, has a different shape—because of course the arches are all different. If you spend a moment thinking about the planning effort this must have involved, you can end up getting quite dizzy and you may have to sit down on the leather-upholstered bench at the point where the now invisible arch reaches the valley. While there, your eye falls on the neatly dovetailed joins of the bench, and the word "flawless" comes to mind. That is how all the carpentry in the building is. The floors, the walls, the ceilings—everything. Piano was deeply impressed by the Swiss craftsmen.

The high glass wall to the west gives the building a clear front and back. As with the wall in Riehen, there is a preferred direction in which to face. One looks toward the city, to Bern. The sun shields

Not until a gray box rises into the glass cube do you realize it is an elevator. There are no rails or pulleys here.

mounted outside do, however, interrupt the view. While the glass corridors are like balconies with dual views, the foyers are interior spaces—a fact that underlines the alternation of broad and narrow in the series of rooms.

Now you understand why the façade is divided into two parts, with the upper part set back slightly. This creates niches for museum use. "Street," by the way, is meant quite literally here. A central path is kept clear, while allowing access to the facilities set up to the left and right: stands, elevators, stairways, and other service facilities. The oak parquet, laid lengthwise along the street, emphasizes its proportions. The curved lines in the floor pattern appear to stretch the 150-meter-long interior street even further. If the Center is open, the locals can incorporate Museum Street into their daily stroll. It is open to anyone—the ticket and security checks do not come until you reach the entrances to the halls.

The elevator in Middle Hill—often overlooked by first-time visitors—demonstrates how one can take things to perfection. Four vertical glass panels form a transparent cube, open at the top, with a metal frame set into its front. What is it for? Not until a sharply outlined gray box rises from below and pushes quietly into the cube do you say to yourself: elevator. There are no rails, no pulleys, no cables—nothing that would indicate that this is an elevator. You think about the inventive genius needed to make an invisible elevator! Anyone who still believes Piano is a high-tech architect, determined to exploit any opportunity to demonstrate his mechanics, ought to take a closer look. Piano is also an architect of effects, and he chooses his methods with care. Here, he suppresses all the technology because he does not want to interrupt the space.

The Holy of Holies is Profane

The heart of the Center is the museum, so the big exhibition hall is the key room. During construction, this room looked like an aircraft hangar—and art lovers wondered anxiously what would happen to the work of Klee when displayed within it.

The argument went round and round in endless repetition: Klee's small-format paintings needed intimacy, and would be lost in a huge hall. Piano did not listen. The hills were more important to him than the grumbling of colleagues. "I have never believed that small works of art require small rooms. The window through which Klee looked upon the world was small, but his own world was large."[26]

Upon entering the 1,620-square-meter hall through the central door, you realize that another world begins here. The background noise drops from loud to quiet, from bazaar to church. The dividing wall between Museum Street and the exhibition room also divides two different atmospheres—the profane and the sacred. Piano said this would be the place where you would want to take your shoes off before entering the holy of holies. The architect is no sober Swiss protestant, he did not fear to give the room a consecrated air. Those who enter should involuntarily start to whisper. Piano also used the metaphor of deceleration: outside on the freeway you drive past in fifth gear; on Museum Street you travel in second; and here, you can only go in first. Apart from the doors, the dividing wall has no other openings, because it is also a security barrier. A museum is a high-security zone.

The first feeling you get when entering is that you have walked out of the sunlight into the twilight. The Building Workshop thought long and hard about light and illumination, simulating the various moods using countless models. The obvious comparison with the Fondation Beyeler is not really appropriate—for Klee's highly sensitive works, most of them watercolors, cannot be exposed to light of an intensity any greater than 50 to 100 lux, or they will fade. The paintings at the Fondation Beyeler, by contrast, can withstand 240 lux. At first, Piano planned to put in skylights, but later realized that that would not be possible. Thus, there is purely artificial light and no light machine. The eye adjusts quickly and begins to take in its surroundings. In the main room, the basic lighting was installed in the vaulted roof; it illuminates the space indirectly via the ceiling. Each painting is highlighted by a spotlight suspended from the ceiling. The lighting is simple, visible, and without forced sophistication. The exhibition space is divided up using screens suspended on cables from the ribs of

The documentation of the project is part of its development. The Renzo Piano Building Workshop shows off what it can achieve.

The oak floor contains openings for the air conditioning as decorative scars. Its lines are inside reminders of the curve of the freeway outside the building.

the roof. They are purely linear elements, which do not touch the walls and never meet to form a corner. The space flows unhindered, unbroken by the creation of smaller spaces. The fact that the dividers hover four centimeters above the ground serves to underline their impermanence. All the fixtures are suspended, descending from above. Over them, hanging on specially developed metal profiles, are rectangular frames with white gauze stretched over them called vela. They allow the light through but are not transparent. These vela transform the hangar into a museum by dividing the vertical space into two zones but nevertheless allowing the visitor to perceive it as a whole. You feel the unified space while still experiencing a certain intimacy in front of the paintings. After all the sequences of closed rooms since the Staatsgalerie Stuttgart, Piano returns to the large, single room. And yet, he keeps the individual, intimate sections of space and the overall space in a mysterious state of flux. He cites the Impressionist notion of "vaporeux."

"In the first moment the architecture really does draw all the attention to itself: under the broad arcs of the steel supports, the room is full of suspended rails, wires, and cables—so that you almost feel you are in a circus tent and that any moment the trapeze artists will make their appearance. But as time passes, all that pulls further and further away into the background."[27]

Renzo Piano predicted just that: "When you come in, you perceive the whole space, but when you start looking at the paintings, you concentrate and find yourself in a much smaller world, without forgetting the whole. [...] Both happen at the same time, like a cosmos and a micro-cosmos. I don't want to theorize, because I am no theorist, but Klee's work contains both—the cosmos and the micro-cosmos. The interplay of big and small creates this drifting atmosphere."[28]

And yet, the ambivalence remains. "The space is ambivalent, but in art ambivalence is not a bad thing because it means many-sidedness,"[29] Piano explains. Architects shake their heads, museum visitors don't worry about it—they look at the paintings. One thing is not ambivalent—Klee's works retain their aura; there is no contextual link between the small formats and the size of the room they hang in. But the mood is not a sacred one—rather it is one of cheerful homage, a prayer room, not a church, profane, not sacred.

"What is the room in Bern made of? A floor, four walls, and the arch of the roof—nothing more. They are the only hard elements, the rest is drifting, nothing more than air. Everything is white. Why? Because white is the color of dreams."[30] The oak parquet we know from the Fondation Beyeler was laid throughout the entire museum. The con-

The height of the rooms is essential. If the exhibition hall were built to the minimum height required, visitors would feel it was pressing down on their heads.

ditioned air comes in through fine slits and is sucked out again at the short end of the hall. These decorative scars in the parquet follow the curve of the façade—and by definition that of the freeway—that is its loose connection with Museum Street; otherwise, the two areas are completely separate. You do not realize how deeply you have penetrated into the slope.

On the lower floor is the hall for temporary exhibitions—a plain rectangular room of 830 square meters in which twelve supports stand. The initial division of the space into an inner area with an outer space to walk around appears to not be the optimum. It was set up this way for the first exhibition using mobile dividers. At the foyer, open to Museum Street, a glass wall forms the end of the room, bringing in natural light. Nevertheless, this too is a room of artificial light. The remarkable thing about it is its height. It is high enough to give the hall volume. It is a room and not just a layer of functional space. The staircase to the lower hall—which one barely takes note of from above—looks dramatic when seen from below, opening up an overly high, narrow space. Once again ambivalence: quiet at the top, powerful at the bottom.

It should be mentioned at this point that these two exhibition rooms can be arranged many different ways—to the delight of the curators. The large halls invite ever-changing elements and experiments. The way they look today is not how they will stay.

More than a Museum

The music, cinema, and lecture hall in North Hill is set deep in the earth. Renzo Piano is experienced in making music venues. For Pierre Boulez he built the IRCAM Project—an institute for research into acoustics and music next to the Centre Pompidou; for Luigi Nono's opera "Prometeo" a music container that could be dismantled. In addition, he made a music and congress hall in the old Fiat factory Lingotto in Turin. In Schöngrün this experience bore fruit. Once more in a closed concrete box, he set an inclined steel framework with some 300 seats that shine red. Horizontal grooves decorate the bare concrete walls, the steel ribs between them have been covered to improve the acoustics. In front of this raw, gray surface, wooden elements are suspended from the ceiling like irregularly mounted panels to ensure the right acoustics, but they also form festive decoration for the room. They have the same color as the seating, and the end of the room behind the orchestra podium is red as well. As ever, Piano has his reasons: "Red is the color of institutions. The red and the velvet remind us of the music and of the concert halls caught

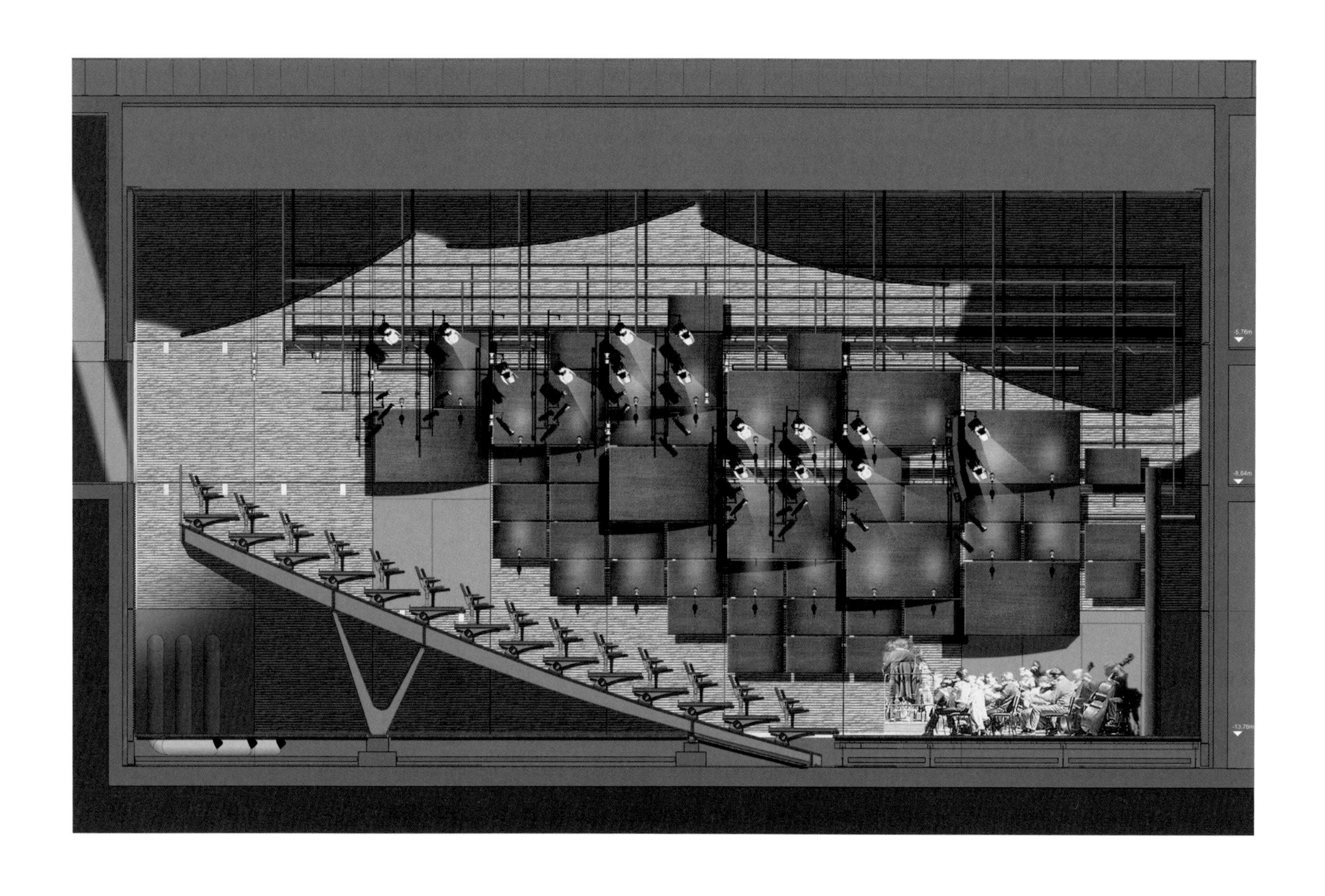

up in our imagination."[31] He would never suggest making a theater white. In all, it is an intimate closed space with a festive atmosphere achieved with purely artificial light. But Piano reminds us: "In a concert hall, mood means primarily the acoustics. Everything depends on that and not on the colors and shapes. Do you ask a Stradivarius about its shape?" He also points out an important condition: "The hall must have a high ceiling, though, or the sound will not live."[32]

It goes without saying that the Auditorium is fitted out with state-of-the-art technology, which can make the sound audible from all sides, isolate or focus it, thereby preparing the hall for cinema, electronic music, or anything else that may come.

The basement of North Hill is home to the children's museum, the Kindermuseum Creaviva. The ground in front of it was removed, creating a garden that ends in a slope. Inside, the Information Zone above it does not reach as far as the façade, making the ceiling twice as high. As a result, you never get the feeling in the children's museum that you are sitting in the basement. There is a workshop atmosphere—playful work is going on.

Piano places lightweight fittings inside the hard concrete box: the metal stand for the audience, the podium, and the wall elements to dampen the sound.

North Hill is also where you find the Forum, a multi-purpose hall with two seminar rooms attached. Without natural light, these rooms appear businesslike and bare; you can use them, but you don't like to stay in them long.
In the Museum Café above, visitors relax in gray and red armchairs at the round green tables. Museum Street, the exhibition halls, the Auditorium, and the Kindermuseum Creaviva are the Center's public areas. Now it is time for a break, and for a visit to the bookshop or the architecture exhibition in the foyer of South Hill.

Behind the Scenes

Of the parts of the Center not open to the public, the Atrium in North Hill is the hidden surprise. The natural light from above and the glass walls that delineate it create a lantern inside the hill. You can look from one of the adjacent workshops, right through the Atrium, to the restoration laboratory opposite. The reflections obscure the spatial divisions, and the transparency allows unexpected views. The staff canteen is located in the Atrium.
South Hill contains an open-plan office, lit by a central skylight. That the approximately forty staff "have to work in their own space, the hill for research and administration, in bare glass cubicles and in some cases narrow niches unvisited by daylight in the lower part of the hill, has so far been accepted without complaint. Visitors here are astonished by the almost cold, seemingly random setup, with open glass dividers and shelves."[33] Building hills means creating difficult spaces whose overheating in summer forces the architect to make subsequent improvements.
In the belly of the building are huge caverns for the technology a museum needs. A modern museum is a closed climate. It is 23 degrees centigrade in summer and 21 degrees centigrade in winter. The permitted deviation is one degree. The humidity is stable, 50 percent, with a permitted deviation of 5 percent. These are the conditions that museums and their insurers require. Questioning them means no works will be lent to you. In order to meet these conditions, huge air conditioning units have been constructed that consume a great deal of energy and are hidden in the depths of the building. But there is method in this madness. That the entire building is very well insulated goes without saying. And, of course, the heating works with a heat recovery function. Put another way—the Zentrum Paul Klee is at the cutting edge of sustainable technology. The building's annual energy consumption will be low in comparison with that of other museums.

The Kindermuseum Creaviva is located on the lower floor but has a link to Museum Street at the façade. One never gets the feeling one is in the basement.

Workshops and the restorers' studios are inside North Hill. They get their light from an Atrium set in the middle.

The Random Functionalist

The project is frankly functionalist as far as its inner organization goes—as always with Piano. Despite the Landscape Sculpture, there is no sentimental green suggestion that this is the womb of mother Earth; this is the realization of a high-tech construction which has been welded together, not stitched. But neither is there a geometric game with sharp angles and sloping walls—Piano builds sensible spaces that fulfill their function.

What do today's museums suffer from? Their overwhelming success. Therefore, they must build for success—and that means for large crowds of visitors. But what is the primary duty of a museum? Protecting, displaying, researching. However, the more visitors it attracts, the greater its recognition. Politicians and the public believe a good museum is one with a line of people at the entrance. Piano solves the contradiction of spectacle and contemplation with his ground plan, which divides up the public areas into different zones. There are basically two of these: the noisy, public, roughly 150-meter-long Museum Street, and behind it—separated by an unbroken wall with matte silver plaster—are the quiet museum halls and workrooms, as well as the Auditorium. The depth of the building becomes a filter. The dividing wall separates the noise of the fair from the spaces of quiet and contemplation. Behind them are the staff-only areas, the workshops, and the stacks. At the very back, in the very innermost part, there is another corridor, closed to the public, which links up these areas.

Each of the three hills has its own function. North Hill is for art education, music, conferences, and the workshops; Middle Hill is for the exhibitions; while South Hill is for research and administration. In summary, it is a rational, functional ground plan.

But while the ground plan is functional, the hills are certainly not. This is the mother of all ambivalence on this project—a functional ground plan is wrapped up in a random sine wave quilt. Put another way, Piano connects a free geomorphic form with a structure organized on strictly functional lines; disciplined organization meets the pathos of the waves. Tension and ambivalence arise from this seeming misalliance.

The new art location is called the Zentrum Paul Klee, not the Klee-Museum. "Zentrum" means more than a museum—a place where more can and should happen than the exhibition of works. It is a multipurpose hall of the arts. It has space for concerts, films, conferences, exhibitions, collections, research, and restoration. A glance at the floor plan shows that the actual exhibition takes up only about one third of the space. Museum Street has become the most important space, and it garners the greatest architectural interest. With the Centre Pompidou Renzo Piano dragged the institution of the museum from the past into the present with one single building. He has done it again here in Bern. He took the museum, which he built in its pure form in Riehen, and turned it into a recreational tool here. The culture industry of the twenty-first century has found its first contemporary production center. It aims to and will succeed in producing far more than contemplation.

The Steel Structure

After the structure, the construction. What remains to be told is how the idea of the three hills was turned into reality.[34] The engineers first thought of a nonaligned shell structure, like the thin concrete membranes of the Burgdorf engineer Heinz Isler, for instance. But when the thin shell is to be given a cladding, the load becomes too great. So the engineers decided to employ a collimated structure. Considerations of how to build it began with the image of ribs, the transverse ribs of a ship's keel. Of what should the supports be made? The engineers left the question open as they tested concrete ribs and various kinds of layered wooden supports, and ultimately arrived at steel. Steel has the advantage of allowing the differing load to be met with differing wall strengths, while the cross section of the girder remains the same. Every arch is different and of varying height, and each is cut out of steel plates with a gas cutting machine, stamped into its final shape, and—because of the high degree of curvature—welded together by hand. Therefore, it did not matter that the shape of the girders was never repeated. With concrete supports, on the other hand, each form could only have been used once.

The first arch (3 in the section of the façade on page 56) has an inclination of nine degrees on the inside. The next five (4a, 4b) rise in a fanlike shape, while all those following stand vertically. This means that the girders and the roof meet at acute angles. The arches are higher than static calculations require, because Piano wanted to show the ribs of the building inside and out. The distance between them of 2.5 meters is quite small for a primary structure but has the advantage of making it possible to outline the hills more precisely. The ribs had to be closer to one another than the optimal structural requirement, because they draw the shape of the wave, as well as the shading on the hills inside and out. Piano was not afraid to extend the girders at the back out into the grass—even if they no longer have a load-bearing function. He needs them to reinforce the landscape.

The image of a ship's hull at the docks provided inspiration from the very beginning. When the hull is turned over it forms a hill.

The planning, manufacture, and mounting of the steel frame were a masterly achievement by the metalworkers.

The task required 330 arch elements made of 1,200 tons of steel and more than 40 kilometers of welds.

Following page: The flatter the arches, the greater the sideways force. Therefore they are set on huge concrete bases.

Francesco della Casa found just the right image: "The building of the ZPK reminds one of Jonathan Swift's benevolent giant Gulliver, rendered immobile by the restraints placed upon him by a multitude of cheerful Lilliputians."[35]

Only the foremost girders run the length of the wave and are stressed together with the aid of tiebacks. Those behind them are braced by compression struts, concrete ribs set into the walls. They have to take up the thrust of the arches, which becomes greater as the curve becomes flatter toward the back. Piano underlined the tiebacks with a heavy base which does not, however, transfer all of the force. The remainder is taken up by a steel wedge set invisibly into the concrete underneath the arch. The base is an expression of the load but in fact bears little of it. "Form follows function" was never Piano's motto; rather he believes that "form follows intention." 1,200 tons of steel were needed, and the metalworkers have welded together more than 40 kilometers of metal seams. 330 arch elements were put in place over six months using 5,000 screws. This was the toughest task steel workers in Switzerland have had to face for a long time. The first prize received by the Zentrum Paul Klee was the Swiss steel construction prize, the "Prix Acier 2005."

The casually drawn waveform had to be translated into geometry so as to be described mathematically. "In order to finally determine the form of the different-sized hills, Piano's office initially employed a method used by Jørn Utzon for the Sydney Opera House (1957–72). All the shells are segments of the same body—in Utzon's case, sections of a sphere; in Piano's sections of a cone."[36] This method allows every point on the shell to be exactly located in three-dimensional space. Just a few short years ago, such a clearly defined but extremely complex form could not have been either planned or produced. The computer made it possible. The 3D-model on the computer became the basis for determining the form, the measurements, and the production of each individual part. You need to imagine the façade as a flat front instead of a curved one in order to fathom what new architectural means of expression the computer has made possible. Piano has always immediately adopted new technology and made architecture out of it.

The Glass Wall

The unusual geometry of the building required the difficult construction of a 150-meter-long glass façade, divided into an upper and a lower section along its entire length. The two sections are marginally offset and connected by the canopy—the roof of Museum Street—

wirz

The sideways force is not taken up by the concrete bases but by the steel ribs running through the valley.

The building has just two faces—the three hills of the roof and the offset glass front along the freeway.

at a height of 4 meters. At its highest point, the façade is 19 meters high, and the largest panes of glass measure 6 by 1.6 meters and weigh 500 kilograms.

The façade and the roof of Museum Street are suspended from four of the roof supports using cables, allowing Museum Street to be free of obstacles. But the movement of the roof is transferred to the façade and must be taken up by a load-bearing system. In the vertical, the roof can move up to seven centimeters, in the horizontal, four. The constructions of the roof and the façade are not inflexible; they have a degree of freedom to move.

The façade is a structural masterpiece in three sections (section of the façade on page 56). Section one: the lower, front façade and the canopy. At the front, it rests on supports; at the back, it is held up by steel cables which are attached to the third and seventh arches (3b, 5). Section two: the upper façade. The force of the wind and the load of its weight are carried by the cables attached half-way up the façade supports. The cables are suspended from a pair of arches (4 and 4b), which ensures a more even distribution of the overall load. The canopy and the upper façade are only linked with one another to distribute the wind load; no vertical forces are transferred. Section three: the balancier. There is no structural link between the fifth arch (4a) and the façade suspended below it. "The supports here meet the so-called balancier, which stands vertically to the façade and is flexibly linked with the roof supports in the axes 4 and 4b."[37] The balancier, the cables, and the supports are pre-stressed, which prevents the cables from losing tension under the wind load.

With the façade, Piano once more demonstrated his mastery of detail. He reveals the layers piled up on top of one another, celebrates the tension-bearing cables, fastening elements, and support bases, and makes the flow of forces visible, demonstrating their mechanics. The visitor is aware of Piano the architect-engineer and engineer-architect—and of his passion. For Piano, perfection is not omission, as with the elevator, it is demonstration. He is a master of both, but German-Swiss minimalism is not his thing; he displays the individual pieces and the coordinated workings of his façade machine. And yet, first impressions can be misleading. The way this façade works can hardly be understood without explanation. Once more, there is ambivalence—things are far more sophisticated than one imagines.

You can see the history of the villa simply by looking at it—the classicist main wing with the 1868 salon on the left and on the right, the old core of the building, dating from the sixteenth century.

La Campagne

The perfect end to your excursion is a visit to the restaurant at Villa Schöngrün, which was noted on arrival. The core of this beautiful old house dates to the middle of the sixteenth century. A barn and a tower were added in the eighteenth century; in 1868, the classicist main building and garden salon came into being. You can still see today how the three epochs fit together.

With heritage comes responsibility. The building has been painstakingly renovated, extended, repaired, and polished as only the preservation-obsessed Swiss can. Each of the rooms today serves as a salon or intimate dining room in the restaurant. This is a stylish place to get married, celebrate a birthday, hold court. You could almost imagine yourself back in the nineteenth century.

Next to the historical building, Piano placed a glass annex, which contains the kitchens at the back and the restaurant at the front. The high-ceilinged room—which is actually a dining room—has something of the greenhouse about it, an industrial elegance. Red chairs are grouped around white tables; white clouds of cloth drift over the guests' heads; horizontal curtains hang in waves on their cords. It is a top-class restaurant of the early twenty-first century with 15 Gault Millau points. These elements serve to emphasize the contrast between the old and the new parts of the building, yet the new permeates the old—the reception area with its bar has settled in on the ground floor. You enter the Restaurant Schöngrün, as one should, via the old main entrance of the villa.

This third major addition is a further chapter in the history of the house and it will not be the last. Villa Schöngrün is a reminder of the "Campagnen," the country residences of Bern's wealthy elite, a reminder of the high-spirited splendor of their summer abodes. Schöngrün could have been the name of a country residence in the novels of Rudolf von Tavel, a Bern dialect writer. The Schnäggenbühl, today called the Luft-Station (Air Station) after a work by Paul Klee, in the nearby cemetery, fits seamlessly in with the continuity of old and new. This artificial hill, whose top is reached via a spiral path, used to serve as a belvedere, offering views of the Bernese Alps. A house from Bern's pre-industrial days stands here. The scent of the ancien régime remains at the villa; it is a scent that will never be banished from Bern.

Quite by chance, the villa is similar in essence to the Zentrum Paul Klee. Because it has atmosphere. Because it is a large building in a large garden, which passes into farmland. Because there are no other properties pressing in on it, no thick hedges necessary to stop the

One of the villa's owners wanted to be able to see the Alps. So he had this lookout hill built.

neighbors peering in—in short, because the Zentrum Paul Klee has been planned on the scale of a country residence. "We mustn't make it small,"[38]—Piano's instinct was right—you can't pack a museum for Paul Klee into a little parcel of leftover land.

The park—or rather, the 2.5-hectare Landscape Sculpture behind the "hills"—is now framed by a drop with steel railings, a reminder of the walls of the castrum lunatum. This draws a border between the sculpture and the surrounding land. A row of birch trees hems the footpath that runs around the edge. The whole area is farming land once more. With each passing season, the park finds an agricultural use. The space is planted uniformly, but the Landscape Sculpture will continually change with the seasons—meadows, corn and fallow fields, freshly ploughed ground, sunflowers or canola. Bern will be the first city to employ an artist farmer.

Paul Klee never became a Swiss citizen, but now the city of Bern has adopted him as its new patron saint. Around the Center, eighteen paths and roads bear names derived from titles of his works: Rad-Wahn (Wheel Mania), unheilige Eile (Harmful Haste), or warum zu Fuss? (Why on Foot?) and Insula dulcamara for instance. The bus loop is at Undo-endo.

And as you sit contentedly in the Restaurant Schöngrün, you should not forget to raise your glass to Maurice E. Müller and Martha Müller-Lüthi. Altogether they have donated some 100 million Swiss francs to the Zentrum Paul Klee. An investment worthy of emulation. It is certainly better than any inheritance.

1 Werner Blaser, Renzo Piano Building Workshop, Museum Beyeler (Wabern-Bern, 1998), p. 137.
2 Renzo Piano, Mein Architektur-Logbuch (Ostfildern-Ruit, 1997), p. 7.
3 Ibid., p. 264.
4 Rudolf Burger, "Die Menschen werden dieses Gebäude lieben, Interview mit Renzo Piano," in Bund, July 18, 2005.
5 Ibid.
6 Piano 1997 (see note 2), p. 12.
7 Blaser 1998 (see note 1), p. 43.
8 Ibid., p. 43.
9 Ibid.
10 Piano 1997 (see note 2), p. 10.
11 Ibid., p. 11.
12 Ibid.
13 Blaser 1998 (see note 1), p. 137.
14 "Ein Ort der Hoffnung, ein Gespräch mit Renzo Piano, Fred Zaugg," in Der Kleine Bund, January 27, 2001.
15 Blaser 1998 (see note 1), p. 47.
16 Zentrum Paul Klee, special supplement to Hochparterre. Zeitschrift für Architektur und Design, no. 12 (Zurich 1999) p. 3.
17 Ibid., p. 4.
18 Ibid., pp. 4 f.
19 Der kleine Bund, January 27, 2001 (see note 14).
20 Zentrum Paul Klee (see note 16), p. 5.
21 Castrum lunatum refers to a Roman fortress such as the one that once stood in Solothurn (Switzerland). It is characterized by a crescent-shaped ground plan with its ends facing the river and its arc facing the land.
22 Der kleine Bund, January 27, 2001 (see note 14).
23 "Paul Klee im schwebenden Raum, Interview mit Renzo Piano," in Hochparterre. Zeitschrift für Architektur und Design, nos. 6/7, 2005, p. 42.
24 Der kleine Bund, January 27, 2001 (see note 14).
25 Gebaute Topografie, Zentrum Paul Klee. Steeldoc 02/05, Bautendokumentation des Stahlbauzentrums Schweiz (Zurich 2005), p. 4.
26 Hochparterre 6/7, 2005 (see note 23), p. 42.
27 Samuel Herzog, "Eine kulturelle Wellnesszone," NZZ, June 18/19, 2005.
28 Hochparterre 6/7, 2005 (see note 23).
29 Ibid., p. 42.
30 Ibid., p. 43.
31 Ibid.
32 Ibid.
33 Lore Dietzen, "Gross und Klein, Das Zentrum Paul Klee," in Bauwelt 32, August 19, 2005, p. 19.
34 Information from Steeldoc 02/05 (see note 25).
35 Francesco della Casa, "Le Centre Paul Klee, ou le paradoxe de Gulliver," in Tracés, no. 18, September 21, 2005.
36 Steeldoc 02/05 (see note 25), p. 4.
37 Ibid., p. 12.
38 Der kleine Bund, January 27, 2001 (see note 14).

The Zentrum Paul Klee and the Surrounding Area

1 Luft-Station
2 Parking lot
3 Bus station
4 Farmhouse
5 Villa Schöngrün and restaurant
6 North Hill
7 Middle Hill
8 South Hill
9 Landscape Sculpture Tour
10 Farmland
11 Main entrance to the Zentrum Paul Klee
12 Pedestrian road Monument im Fruchtland
13 Freeway A6
14 Sculpture Park
15 Hill and birch grove
16 Soundproofing embankment
17 Pedestrian bridge

6
7
8
9
11
12
13
14
15
16
17
575
570

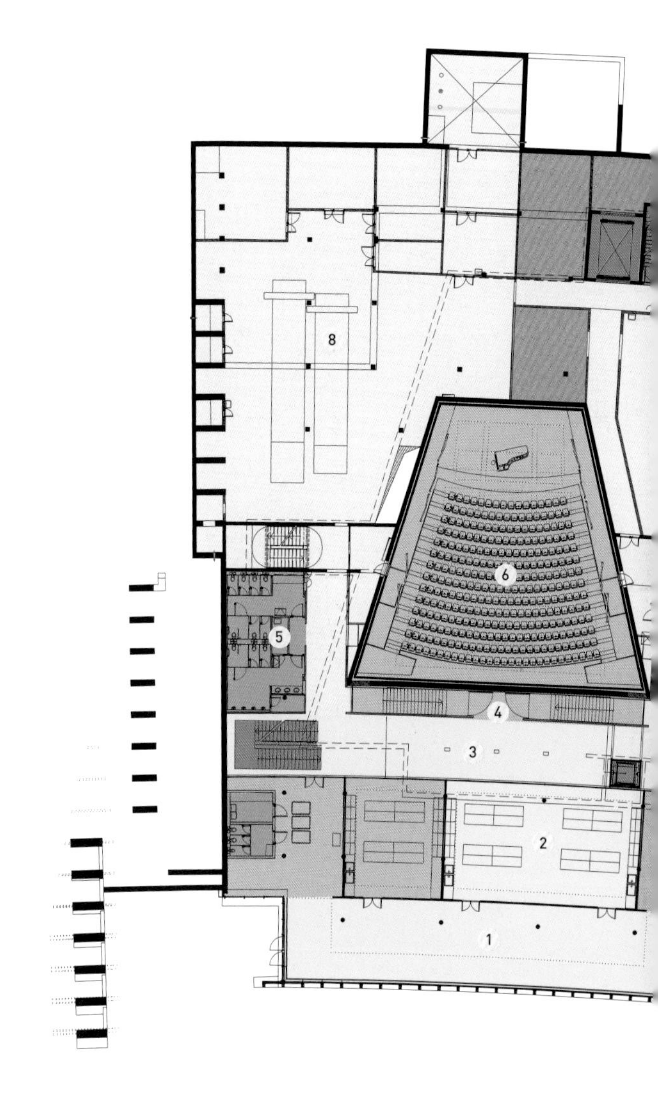

Basement (Lower Level 1)

1 Loft Kindermuseum Creaviva
2 Kindermuseum Creaviva
3 Foyer of the Auditorium
4 Entrance to the Auditorium
5 Toilets
6 Auditorium
7 Checkrooms
8 Building services
9 Connecting walkway
10 Museum storeroom
11 Foyer of the temporary exhibitions area
12 Temporary exhibitions area

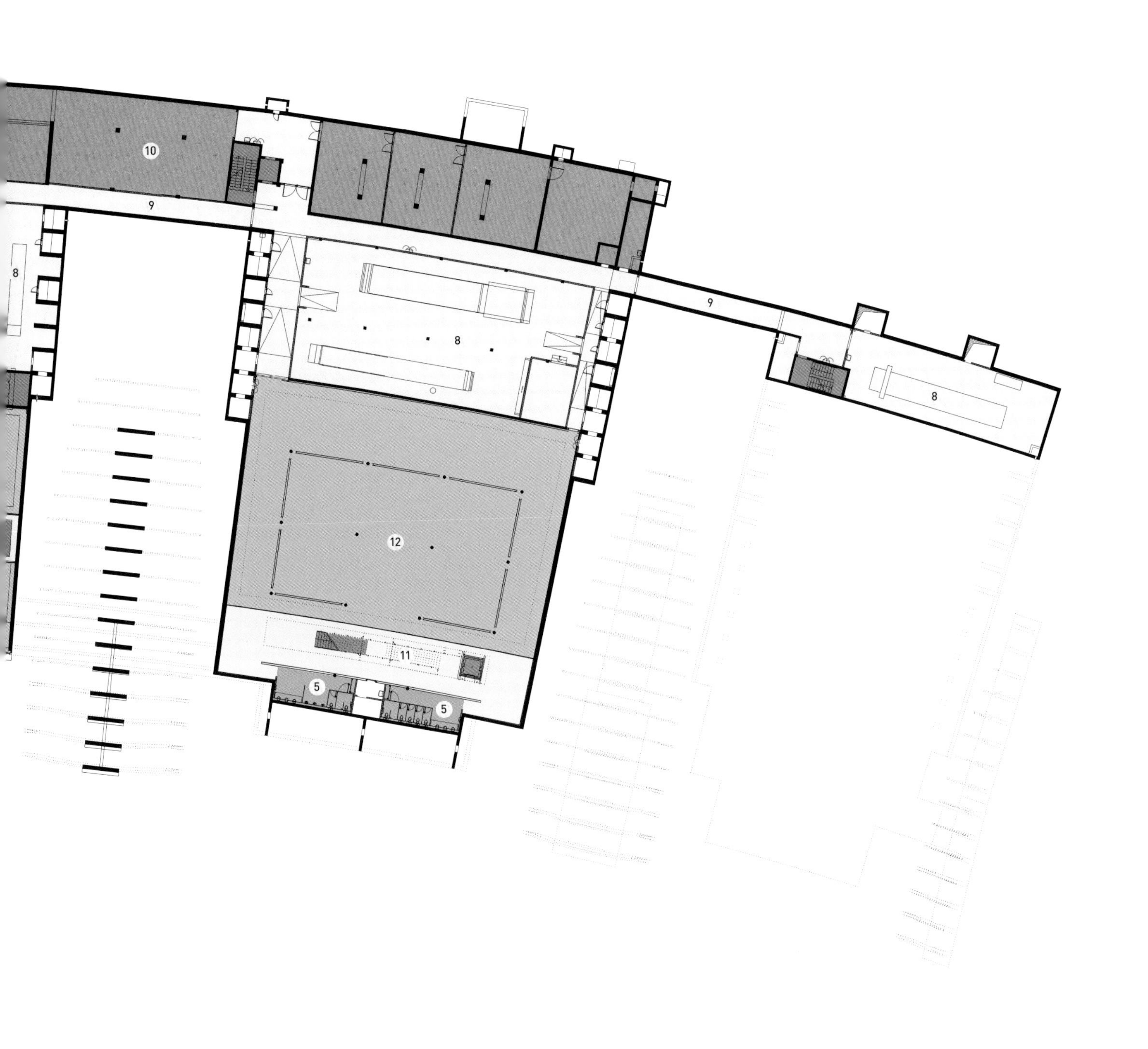
10
9
8
8
9
8
12
11
5
5

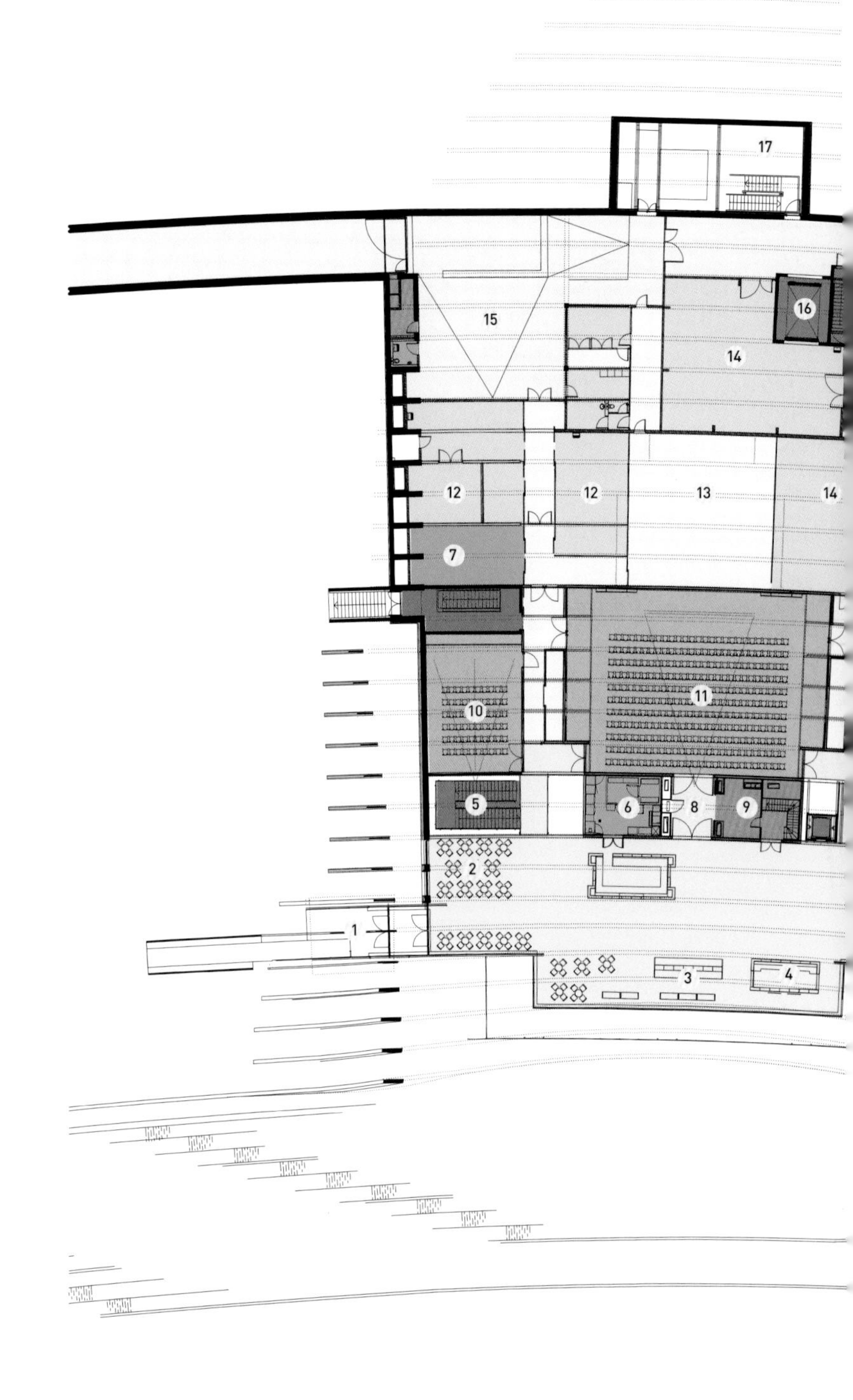

Ground Floor

1 North exit to the Restaurant Schöngrün
2 Museum Café
3 Information desk
4 Ticket Office
5 Stairs to the Auditorium and Kindermuseum Creaviva
6 Catering kitchen (Café)
7 Catering kitchen (Forum)
8 Entrance to the Forum
9 Conference office
10 Seminar rooms
11 Forum (multi purpose hall)
12 Workshops
13 Atrium
14 Restoration studio
15 Delivery area
16 Goods elevator
17 Building services
18 Access bridge
19 Main entrance
20 Valley garden
21 Storeroom
22 Internal service corridor
23 Museum Shop
24 Stairway to temporary exhibitions area
25 Presentation of the collection
26 Museum Street
27 Reading area for visitors
28 Offices for research and administrative staff
29 Service rooms
30 South entrance

22
21
22
29
25
20
20
28
26
19
24
10
23
10
26
18
27
30

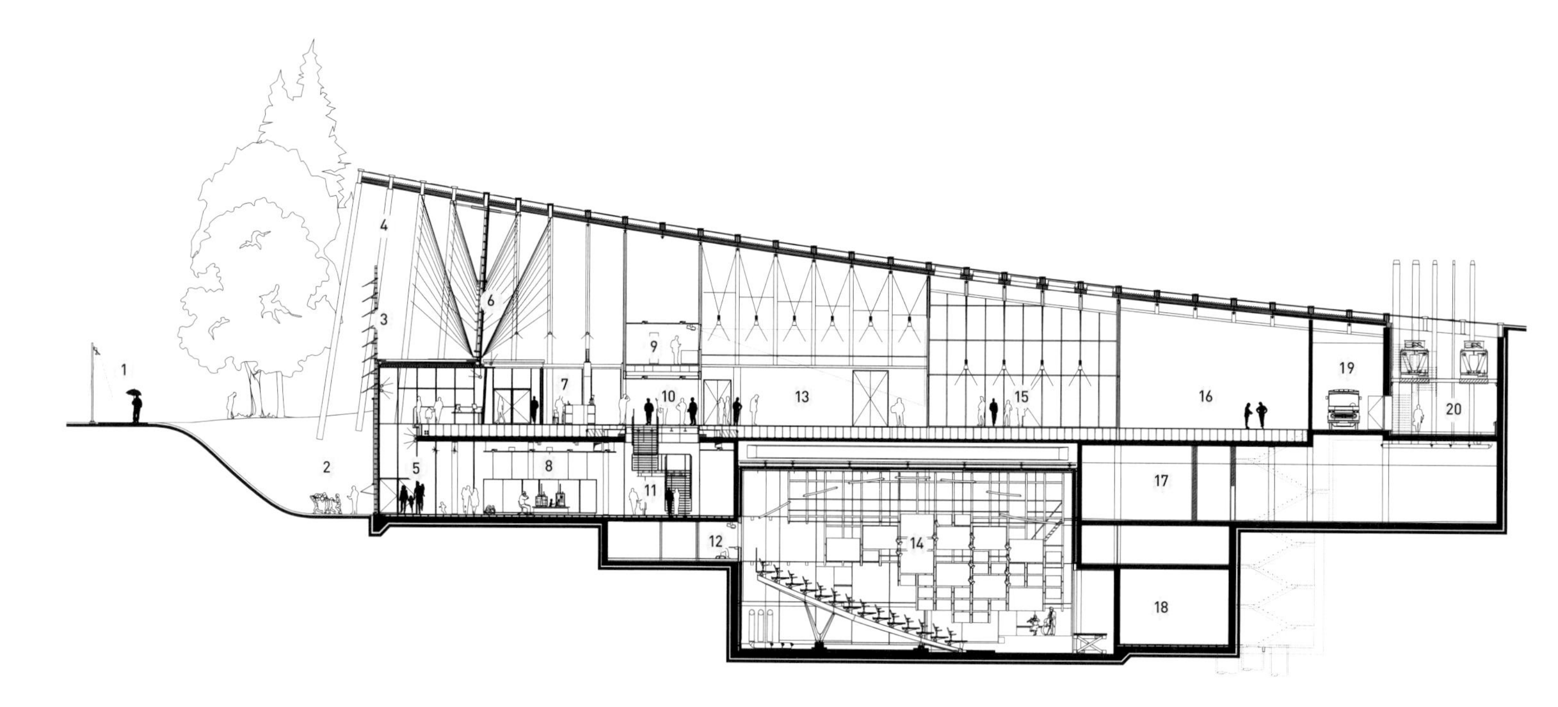

Cross-section of the North Hill

1 Pedestrian road Monument im Fruchtland
2 Garden of the Kindermuseum Creaviva
3 Awning
4 Steel girder
5 Loft Kindermuseum Creaviva
6 Main façade, suspended and set back
7 Museum Street with Ticket Office and Information Desk
8 Kindermuseum Creaviva
9 Forum control room
10 Entrance to the Forum
11 Foyer of the Auditorium
12 Auditorium control room
13 Forum (multi-purpose hall)
14 Auditorium
15 Atrium
16 Restoration studio
17 Building services
18 Backstage
19 Delivery area
20 Building services

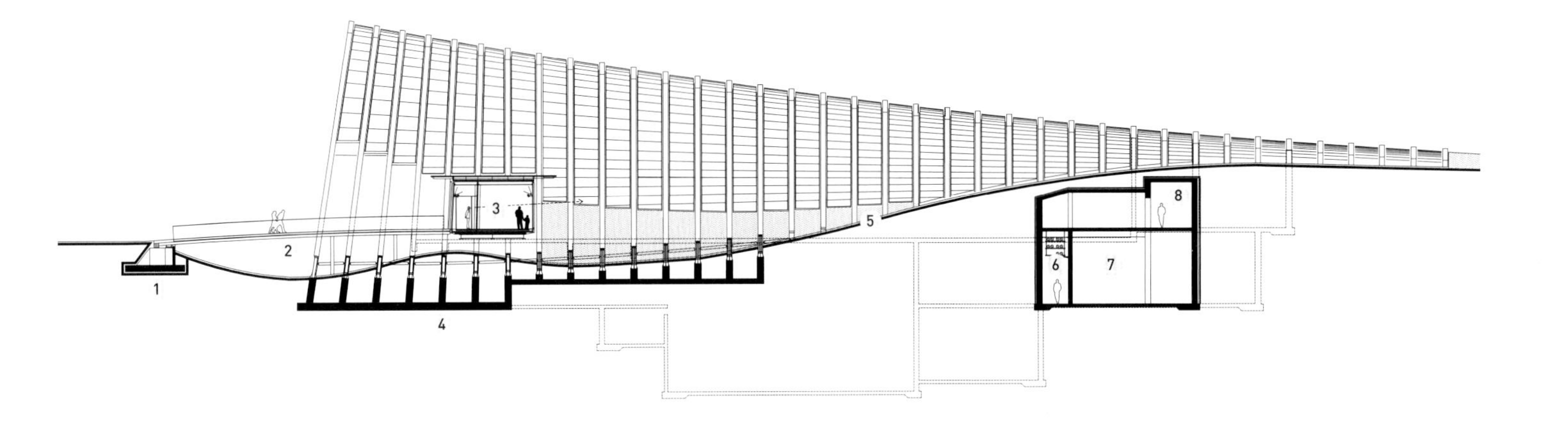

Cross-section valley between North and Middle Hill

1 Bridge foundations
2 Access bridge
3 Main entrance and Museum Street
4 Supports for the steel girders
5 Terrain contour
6 Access corridor
7 Storerooms
8 Service corridor

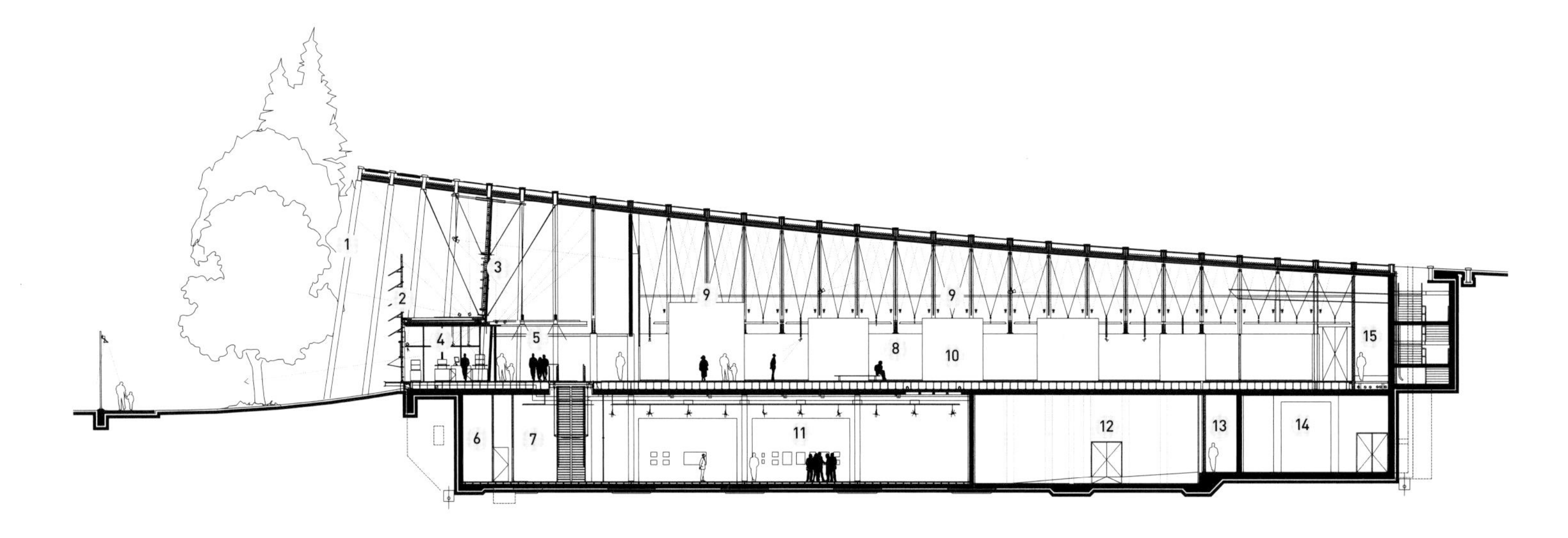

Cross-section of the Middle Hill

1 Steel girder
2 Awning
3 Main façade, suspended and set back
4 Museum Shop
5 Museum Street
6 Toilets
7 Foyer of the temporary exhibitions area
8 Presentation of the collection
9 Velum
10 Suspended walls
11 Temporary exhibitions area
12 Building services
13 Corridor
14 Museum storeroom
15 Internal service corridor

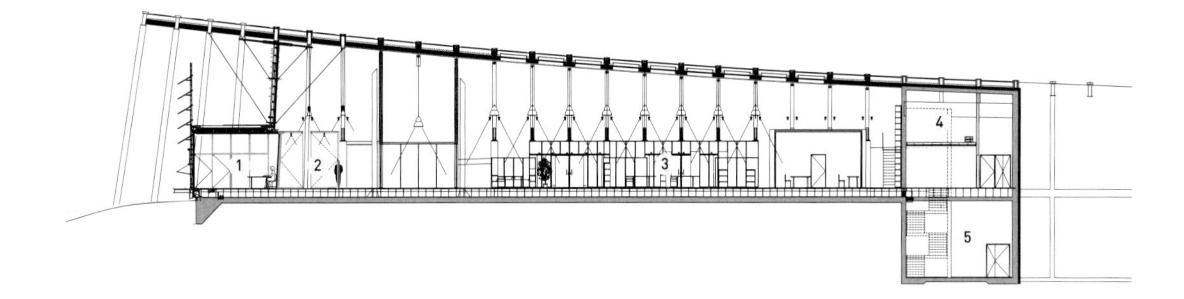

Cross-section of the South Hill

1 Reading area for visitors
2 Museum Street
3 Offices for research and administrative staff
4 Service rooms
5 Building services

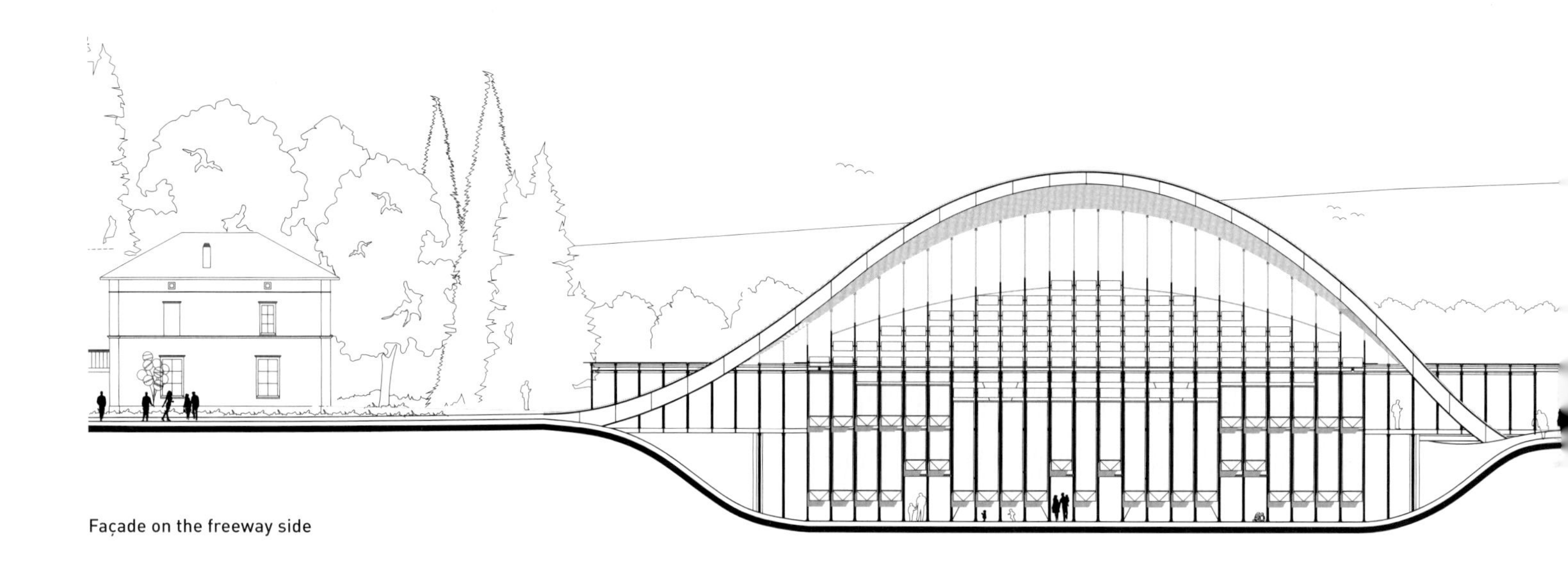

Façade on the freeway side

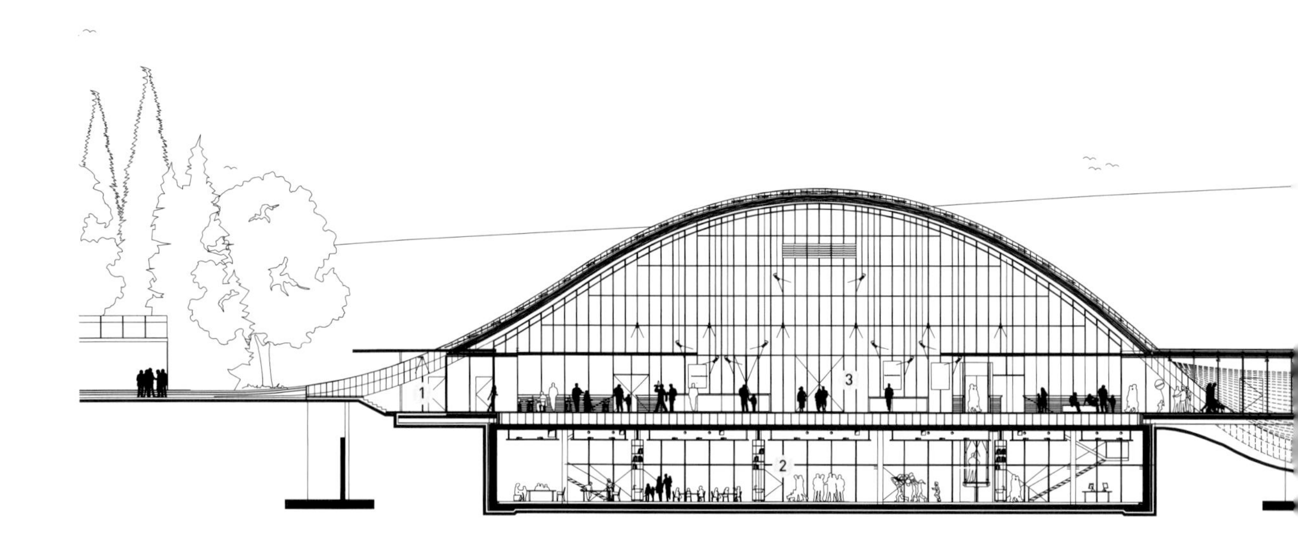

Longitudinal section of Museum Street

1 North exit to the Restaurant Schöngrün
2 Kindermuseum Creaviva
3 Museum Street
4 Foyer of the temporary exhibitions area
5 Entrance of the permanent collection area
6 Glass elevator
7 South entrance

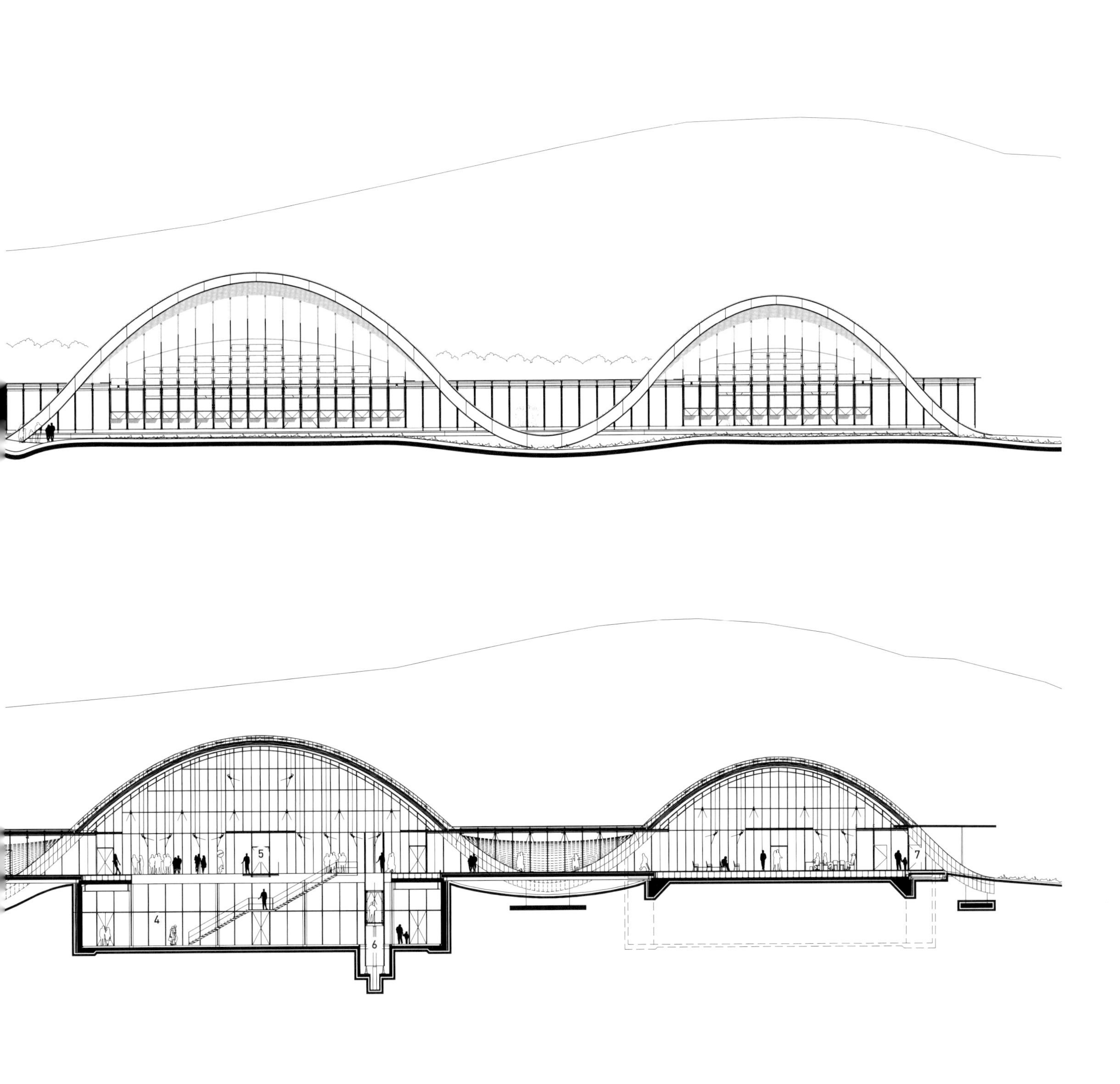
5
7
4
6

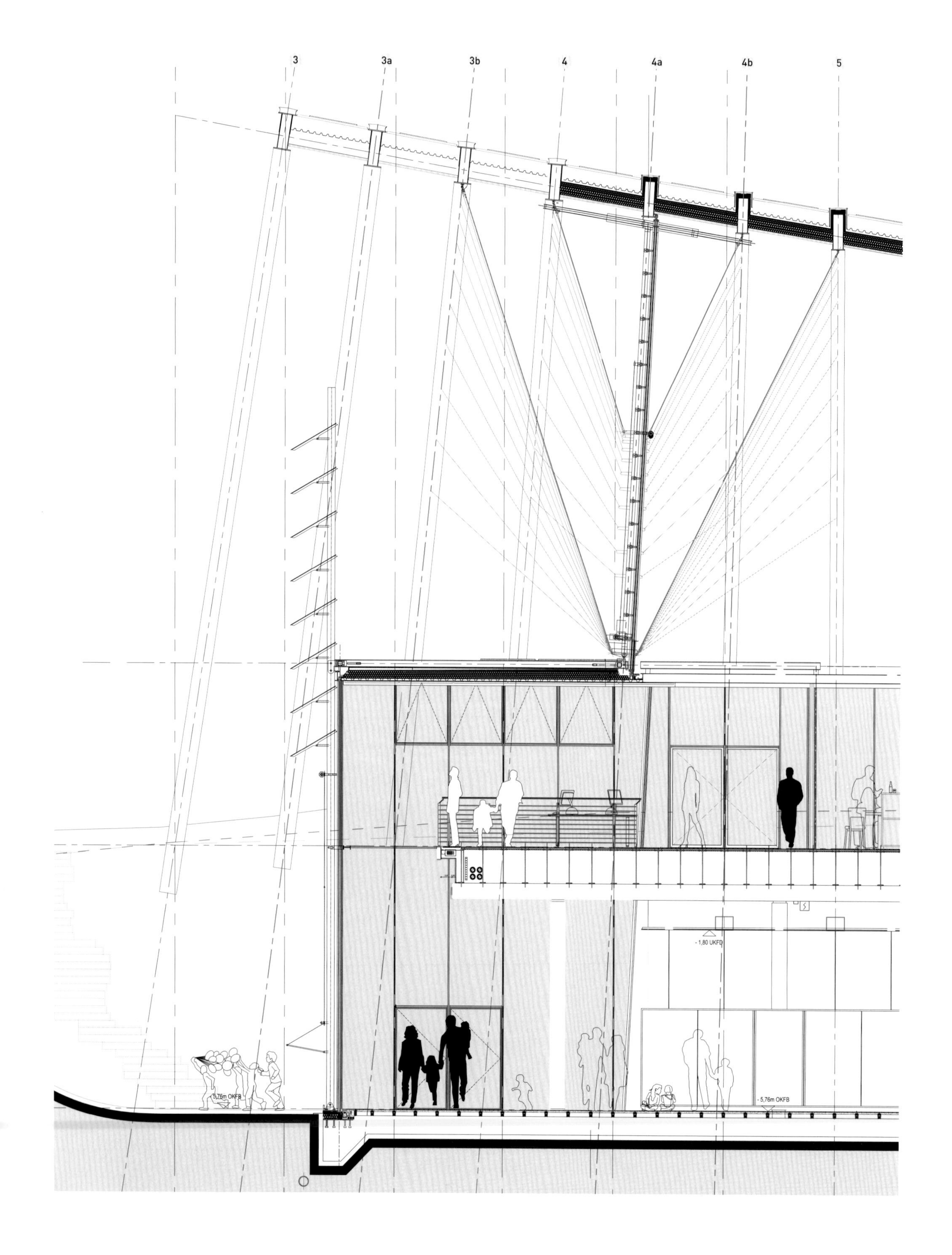
3
3a
3b
4
4a
4b
5
- 1,80 UKFD
- 5,76m OKFB
- 5,76m OKFB

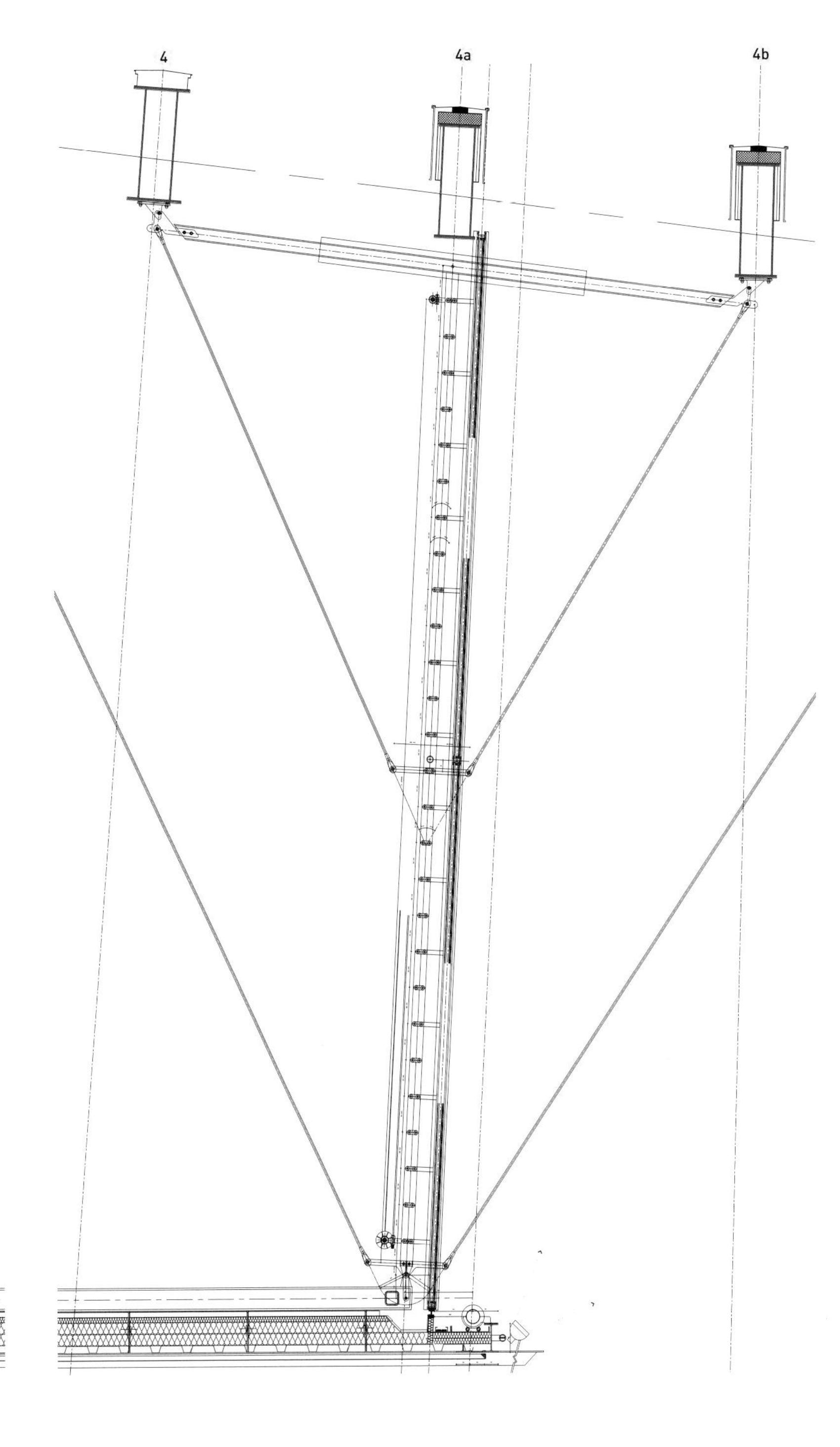

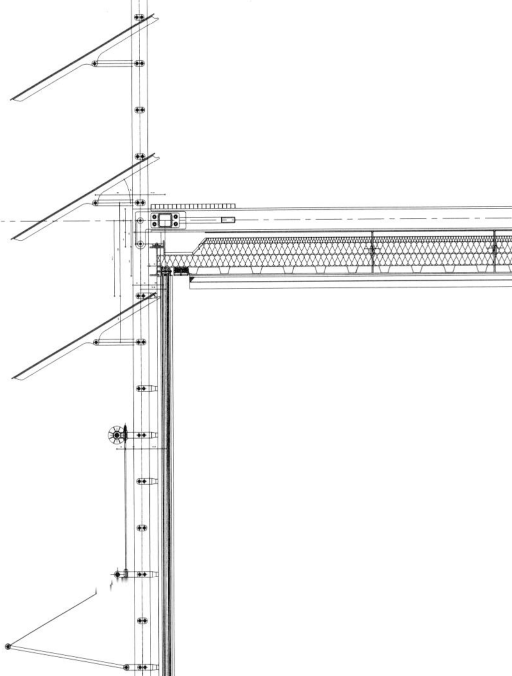

Preceding page: Cross section of the façade at the middle of North Hill. The first six girders have been inclined inwards in a fan shape; the seventh is vertical.

Left detail: The front of the canopy rests on the façade supports, at the back it is held up by steel cables attached to ribs 3b and 5.

Right detail: The balancier takes up the supports, forming a flexible link between ribs 4 and 4b. There is no structural link with rib 4a.
The upper façade is suspended from cables attached to ribs 4 and 4b. No vertical forces are placed on the canopy.

The mid section of a girder is put in place in the valley. The continuity of the ribs and their concrete bases can be seen clearly.

In order to assemble the arches the steel workers constructed a moveable bridge. It is amazing how few people were needed to perform this difficult task.

Following pages: The long row of ribs reminds one of the original image used: the transverse ribs of an upside-down ship's keel.

The steel rib construction of the three hills shortly before the topping out ceremony, the last arches of North Hill are still missing.

It is not only the steel construction that is enormous. To build it also required moving enormous amounts of earth using huge construction equipment and transportation vehicles.

Once the steel construction was in place the less spectacular construction of the roofs of the hills and the roof cladding could begin.

The ribs grow "naturally" out of the ground. You forget that their ends no longer have a load-bearing function.

The interior of South Hill before the floor was put in. The under-floor ventilation channels are still freely accessible.

The exhibition hall of the permanent collection in Middle Hill prior to the floors being installed. The huge space looks like a sports hall.

Chronology and Construction Details

1940	June 29: Paul Klee dies in Locarno
1946	September 20: Hermann Rupf and Dr. Hans Meyer-Benteli purchase the estate Rolf Bürgi is the sole agent September 22: Lily Klee dies in Bern September 24: Klee-Gesellschaft established
1947	September 30: Paul-Klee-Stiftung established
1952	December: Accord between the Paul-Klee-Stiftung and Felix Klee
1990	August 13: Felix Klee dies
1993	Alexander Klee calls for the construction of a museum
1994	April 29: Mayor Dr. Klaus Baumgartner proposes a schoolhouse, the old Progymnasium, as a location
1997	Livia Klee-Meyer Donation Agreement with public authorities
1998	July 7: Announcement that Maurice E. Müller has donated 30 million at least (encumbered with a charge) August: Feasibility study for Lorraine bridge site November 3: Permanent loan contract with Alexander Klee [signed] November 4: Contract for Klee center [signed] November 4: Maurice E. and Martha Müller Foundation established December 18: Renzo Piano commissioned to design the museum
1999	December 9: Exhibition of project proposals at the Kornhaus
2000	September 15: Paul-Klee-Stiftung becomes the Stiftung Zentrum Paul Klee November 27: Bern Canton parliament approves the project: 132 in favor, 7 against November 30: Bern City Council approves the project: 66 in favor, 0 against
2001	March 4: Referendum in the city of Bern: 78 % in favor October 15: First earth turned October 18: Building permit issued
2002	June 20: Foundation stone laid
2003	December 1: Topping-out ceremony
2005	June 20: Public allowed to visit for the first time June 21: Official opening and handover of the building to the Stiftung Zentrum Paul Klee

Further details available in: Zentrum Paul Klee, Bern (Ostfildern-Ruit, 2005).

Construction Details

Title: Zentrum Paul Klee, Bern, CH
Location: Monument im Fruchtland 3, 3006 Bern, CH
Client: Maurice E. and Martha Müller Foundation, Bern, CH
Construction board: Ueli Laedrach, studied architecture at the Swiss Federal Institute of Technology
Project: Renzo Piano Building Workshop (RPBW), Paris, F
Project Director RPBW: Bernard Plattner, studied architecture at the Swiss Federal Institute of Technology
Project team: Morten Busk-Petersen, Oliver Hempel (responsible architects), with Joost Moolhuijzen (partner) and Attila Eris, Mauro Prini, Luca Battaglia, Francesco Carriba, Loïc Couton, Serge Drouin, Olivier Foucher, Herbert Gsottbauer, Florian Kohlbecker, Joon Paik, Dominique Rat, Anke Wollbrink (architects) Roman Aebi, Olivier Aubert, Christophe Colson, Florian de Saint-Jouan, Pierre Furnemont, Yiorgos Kyrkos (models)
Coordination, site management: ARB working group, qualified architects SIA BSA, Bern, CH
Project direction ARB: Kurt Aellen, studied architecture at the Swiss Federal Institute of Technology
Coordination and site management: Mario Ricklin, Alain Krähenbühl, Mauro Pompizi, Gerhard Schläfli, Patrizia Hofer, and Alex Szankasy
Construction period: October 2001 – June 2005

Specialist Planners

Structure: Ove Arup International Ltd., London, GB, with B+S Ingenieur AG, Bern, CH / A. Walz, Stuttgart, D (geometric calculations) / Ludwig & Weiler, Augsburg, D (statics, special elements)
Technical equipment: Ove Arup with LUCO AG, Bern, CH (air conditioning/climate control)
Ove Arup with Enerconom AG, Bern, CH (heating/cooling/sanitary facilities) / Ove Arup with Bering AG, Bern, CH (electrical)
Light: Ove Arup with Bering AG, Bern, CH
Façades: RPBW with Emmer Pfenninger Partner AG, Münchenstein, CH
Building physics: Grolimund & Partner AG, Bern, CH / Müller-BBM, Planegg, D (Auditorium acoustics)
Security: Hügli Ingenieurunternehmung AG, Bern, CH
Fire safety: Institut de Sécurité, Neuchâtel, CH
Signage: Coande. Network for Communication and Design, Zurich, CH
Landscape: RPBW with Swiss School of Agriculture, Zollikofen, CH, and Franz Vogel, Bern, CH

Type of Construction

Ground and lower floors: reinforced concrete
Roof-bearing structure: reinforced concrete with curved, welded arch girders
Façade: steel/aluminium/glass façade, suspended on cables
Roof and support cladding: CNS metal

Execution

Master building work: ARGE Wirz AG/Ramseier AG/Büchi AG/Frutiger AG, Bern, CH
Steel construction: Zwahlen + Mayr AG, Aigle, CH
Façades: Tuchschmid AG, Frauenfeld, CH
Roof: ARGE Ramseyer + Dilger / Ediltecnica AG, Bern, CH

Project data (SIA 416)

Property size GSF: 89,020 m^2 (59,970 m^2 area of Landscape Sculpture)
Base area: 9,760 m^2
Net floor area: 13,587 m^2

Building costs

Total cost: 110 m CHF

Contributors

Canton Bern (Lottery Fund): 18 m CHF
Maurice E. and Martha Müller Foundation: 60 m CHF
Founding partners and patrons: 32 m CHF

With its donation of part of the land, the provision of services, and a development loan the City and the Canton of Bern provided 40 million Swiss francs in assistance.
The operating costs of some 9 million francs annually will be covered by sales at the Zentrum Paul Klee and by contributions from the Canton, the City, and Local Authorities of the Region
The Civic Community of Bern set up a Foundation with capital of 20 million, which assists the Zentrum Paul Klee at short notice with the purchase of works, exhibitions, and in covering the expenses for special events. This would not otherwise have been possible.

"My job was to create a place which corresponds to the spirit of Paul Klee, who was exceptional in his simplicity and creativity."

Renzo Piano

Zentrum Paul

Preceding pages: The freeway is still hidden from view in its trench, but the noise of traffic makes it clear—you are on the edge of a town.

Villa Schöngrün and the three waves are linked by a path. It bears the name of a Klee painting: Monument im Fruchtland (Monument in the Fertile Country).

To house the restaurant a greenhouse-like annex was built onto the villa, thus adding a fourth phase of building to the previous three.

The salon has a view of North Hill. Like Gulliver in Lilliput, the huge body is tied to the ground with countless ropes.

Is the wave sinking into the ground, or is it rising up out of it?
The transition from the building to the grounds is veiled,
and will eventually become even more overgrown.

The restaurant's new annex is a high-ceilinged, bright room, a dining room with the aloof charm of industrial elegance.

The four phases of the Villa's construction: twenty-first-century restaurant, eighteenth-century tower, sixteenth-century core, and the classicist main wing built in 1868.

A steel profile forms the frame of the Landscape Sculpture. The border between the castrum lunatum and the landscape is precisely drawn.

The ensemble of the Villa Schöngrün retains an air of the summer residence it once was for a wealthy patrician family of Bern during the Ancien Régime.

Following pages. A view of the countryside around Bern. The long spine of the Gurten forms the horizon. It is a sandstone hill, carved by the Aare glacier.

How long have these hills been here? Since the last ice age—
or only since 2005? The Zentrum Paul Klee is not a building,
it is a Landscape Sculpture.

The sculpture is fertile. An art farmer nurtures, plows, sows, and harvests. The color and the texture change with the rhythm of the seasons.

The Sculpture Park is a place for quiet and contemplation.
You stroll along meandering gravel paths past works by
Wiggli, Penalba, and Dana.

Even before the construction of the Center, there was an artificial lake between the neighboring 1980s residential area and the Zentrum Paul Klee.

You need to imagine the façade as a flat front against the background of the freeway in order to realize the creative possibilities the computer offers the architect.

Following pages: What computers can do. Without a machine to order, analyze, and draw, the complex geometric forms could not have become reality.

The freeway is a vital artery of the city. The Zentrum Paul Klee turns toward it, not away. Its curve governs the ground plan.

The serpentines rest on exposed roots, plants creep underneath this disciplined tumult. This view has become a favorite with photographers.

What was originally intended to be an earth mound has become a structured wave. The ribs fill in the hatching of the Landscape Sculpture.

Labiler Wegweiser (Unstable Signpost) is the title of a Klee watercolor done in 1937. Piano took it literally and put one up near the entrance.

Following pages: The valley at the main entrance runs under the walkway of Museum Street. The transparent glass path perforates the closed side of the hill.

Sammlung
Shop
Auditorium
Foyer
Zentrum Paul Klee,
Forschung, Verwaltung,

Preceding pages: The valley as a high point—the concept of the hills is most surprising when turned upside down.
The discipline of the detailing becomes very obvious here.

Visitors are not directed, as you might expect, to the northern end of Museum Street, rather, they are guided in an arc into the first valley via a bridge.

All the shapes are sections of a cone. The radius of the façade at the Museum Street level is 500 m.

Following pages: The interplay of closed and transparent shells is intentional and intensifies as you go along. Piano knows how to get the most out of his instruments.

To envision what the computer has to offer in terms of new shapes, the façade must be imagined as straight, not as a curve.

It is the transparency that brings the sculpture to life. The flank of the hill is presented as part of the landscape to visitors on Museum Street.

Two systems interact and reinforce one another—the right-angled tact of the uprights cuts through the flowing arc of the steel ribs.

Inside and out flow into one another—the arches on Museum Street dive down into the ground as if sinking into water.

In the open-plan office, the sun draws charming silhouettes on the wall, but it also heats the room up. Building hills creates difficult spaces.

Desks on the piazza of South Hill make it possible to study or access the internet. Your gaze is drawn to the landscape outside.

Following pages:
Museum Street from the south. The high entrance areas are linked by low-ceilinged glass walkways, creating a series of wide and narrow spaces.

The entrance area in Middle Hill. On the left, the stairs lead down to the temporary exhibitions; on the right is the Museum Shop.

Kein
Tag
ohne
Linie
Nulla
dies
sine
linea
Sammlung
Wechselausstellung

The hall housing the collection in Middle Hill. Dividers suspended from the ceiling turn the room into something between a wide hall and a collection of intimate viewing spaces.

The gauze stretched on frames over some sections of the room serves to divide the space without closing it off.

Your attention is first drawn by the arched roof, but soon you
focus on the pictures in front of you, a much smaller horizon.

"The room is ambiguous, but in art, ambiguity is not a bad thing, because it allows many meanings," says Piano.

One thing is certain—the paintings retain their aura. There is no link between the small size of the pictures and the large size of the room.

The drawn-out curve of the freeway is repeated in the openings for the air conditioning. They are an inside reminder of what is outside.

Museum Street with the piazza in Middle Hill—the change of angle in the façade creates space for the Museum Shop.

Following pages:
Descending the stairs to the room for temporary exhibitions, the visitor does not suspect the surprise which awaits him at the bottom.

Four glass plates, a metal frame, and a railing around it—nothing more. You have to look very closely to discover the elevator, reduced to the absolute minimum.

Surprising space—the temporary exhibitions foyer impresses with its high ceiling, because it incorporates the space of the area above.

At the foyer in the basement, open to Museum Street, a glass wall forms the end of the hall for the exhibitions, bringing in natural light from above.

Kein
Tag
Nulla
dies
sine
linea
Sammlung

Kein
Tag
ohne
Nulla
dies
sine
linea

Sammlung

Nulla
dies
sine
linea

The room for temporary exhibitions on the lower floor is higher than it technically needs to be. But its spaciousness is essential so that you can feel comfortable in it.

Following pages:
What do today's museums suffer from? From their overwhelming success. Museum Street takes on all the functions that the leisure society demands.

The Zentrum Paul Klee is not just a place for researching, displaying, and preserving art; it is also for communicating it. And the Kindermuseum Creaviva is dedicated to doing just that.

Kasse 1
Information
Einlosen Gutscheine

The Zentrum Paul Klee is suited for staging conferences, congresses and meetings. It offers a wide choice of premises for events with 30 to 300 persons (South IV seminar room).

The Forum, a multi-purpose hall, provides a venue for small conventions, lectures, and banquets. The technical facilities are designed to meet any need.

Transparency inside—in North Hill, you can look from the restoration studios right through the Atrium into the workshops.

From the Foyer outside the Auditorium, you can see into the Kindermuseum Creaviva and perceive the world outside. Here, too, the height of the ceiling ensures a comfortable atmosphere.

On the opposite side of the Foyer are the stairs that lead down to the Auditorium. In the background is the staircase to the ground floor

Following pages: The Auditorium may be used as a cinema or lecture hall. The wood panels on the walls and the ceiling ensure perfect acoustics.

View of the building illuminated at night—the Kindermuseum Creaviva below the piazza of North Hill. The blinds create a pattern of lines on the façade.

Following pages: The Zentrum Paul Klee is the modern expression of Bern's self-esteem. The bear of Bern is strong and proud. He has succeeded.

Lifework

In Honor of the Founders Maurice E. Müller and Martha Müller-Lüthi

Dr. Rolf Soiron, Basel

The idea of building a permanent home for Paul Klee's œuvre—designed by none other than Renzo Piano—in the Schöngrün area of Bern, just behind his own house, is one in a series of visions that have driven, accompanied, and even guided him throughout his life, Maurice E. Müller said when he first publicly announced his intention to establish a foundation. Some of these plans, he noted, disappeared into thin air. And even the dreams that would eventually become reality initially met with obstacles, until, often suddenly and unexpectedly, an opportunity presented itself.[1]

In other words, Maurice E. Müller's lifetime achievements did not happen just like that. No, here is a man who has always followed his dreams—and been able to realize them, even when faced with difficulties. The ability not simply to envision but to translate vision into reality is a rare gift. Maurice E. Müller has been adept at recognizing people blessed with this gift and enjoyed surrounding himself with them, regardless of their field of expertise.

Even as a child he dreamed of becoming a surgeon. His father had also wished to pursue this career, emigrating to the United States at a young age and later becoming a physician. But in the end, he had to return to Switzerland to take over the family business in Biel. By contrast, Maurice E. Müller was able to follow his dream, and in doing so found happiness. Indeed, as he himself has said, his life has been so interesting because he has been able to perform surgery all over the world.

Of course, he also dreamed of becoming a good surgeon. He headed large hospitals in Saint Gall and Bern while also working as a university professor. When he set his instruments aside, past the age of eighty, he had performed a total of twenty thousand operations and four thousand hip replacements. There were many grateful patients, some of whom had given up all hope of living without pain or ever using their limbs again.

Had he also dreamed of being the best surgeon of his time? That was precisely the honorary title—Surgeon of the Twentieth Century—he was awarded by the Société Internationale de Chirurgie d'Orthopédie et de Traumatologie (SICOT) in summer 2002. Indeed, the Society's eulogy leaves no doubt about this distinction, proclaiming him "probably the greatest orthopedic surgeon who ever lived."[2] A dozen honorary doctorates and a long series of prestigious awards have only underscored this fact.

There are two accomplishments in particular that have secured him a place in the history of medicine: the dramatic improvement in the treatment of bone fractures, of which he was the driving force and guiding spirit; and progress in the operative treatment of hip and, later, other joint diseases, for which he and his friend Sir John Charnley developed the first reliable methods. These lifetime accomplishments did not simply happen. Starting in 1944, they became his vision and life purpose—one might even say his calling.

With the qualifying examination under his belt, he joined a practice in Bern as a stand-in physician. A patient whose femur had been severed by a falling tree during the Finnish-Russian War in 1940 came to see him for a consultation. A German military doctor by the name of Gerhard Küntscher had treated the injury by inserting an intramedullary pin, and after a mere two weeks the patient had been able to walk with crutches. Now, four years later, he had no complaints, but simply wanted to ask if his implant could be removed. Another patient impressed Maurice E. Müller as well. He could only walk with a cane, and even that required extreme effort, but he did not complain. On the contrary, the hip replacement he had received in Paris two years earlier had relieved him of the unbearable pain he had suffered day and night.

Both cases cast their spell on the twenty-six-year-old. For two weeks he dwelled upon what he had seen and then set out on his course: he wanted to achieve something in these fields. In the decades that followed he would change the world.

At the time, the field of surgery was on the verge of many breakthroughs, able to offer help in a growing number of increasingly difficult cases. But bone fractures remained of little interest, and, characteristically, in the leading hospitals they were typically left to assistants. Skeletal traction, casts, and immobilization were still the standard treatment in most cases. Complications were common, and enforced inactivity proved to be a burden to many patients. The results were entirely unsatisfactory. In 1945, the Swiss insurer SUVA had to pay out permanent disability in 40 percent of cases involving fractures to the lower leg, and in 70 percent of cases involving femur fractures.[3] The prospects for patients with degenerative joint disease were not much better, and more often than not, lifelong pain and severe disability loomed on the horizon. For some time, the medical establishment had experimented with various procedures, but these proved beneficial to only a limited number of patients. A reliable and widely applicable method had yet to be discovered. From this perspective, the course Maurice E. Müller chose makes perfect sense.

In 1944, however, it would have been hard to imagine the urgency with which the world would soon need a solution to these problems. Did Maurice E. Müller perhaps foresee that fractures and joint diseases would, before long, be counted among the world's most common medical problems? Did anyone predict their cause—namely, demographic and social change? Did he suspect that life expectancy would rise so dramatically, or that traditional modes of work, sports, leisure, and communications—and thus behavior and lifestyle—would undergo such fundamental transformations?

Today, respect and gratitude for Maurice E. Müller's lifetime achievements are universal and uncontested. But before reaching this point, he met with numerous obstacles—some of which were difficult to overcome. There was the envy and small-mindedness always encountered by those who accomplish great things. And the young man, as is so often the case, had to deal with the indifference, skepticism, and antagonism of those who had already become part of the establishment. Indeed, as self-evident as Müller's ideas appear to us today, they met with scientific opposition at least into the late 1950s.[4] For a long time, medical authorities in the Anglo-Saxon world stuck to their creed "a closed fracture remains closed." The situation in Switzerland was no better. When Sankt Gallen was recruiting a chief of surgery for the new orthopedic unit in its canton hospital in 1958, Maurice E. Müller was the only applicant to have become a full professor and hold the title of specialist in both surgery and orthopedics. Nevertheless, opposition came from as far away as Zurich, and there were many who believed it necessary to warn against, or even scuttle, his candidacy. They were suspicious of this daring new physician, barely forty years old, with his unconventional methods.

The obstacles Maurice E. Müller encountered never caught him by surprise, however. This is why he always carried his ideas, discoveries, and plans around with him for a long time, ceaselessly questioning them until he was confident of his conclusions. Only occasionally has his bubbling enthusiasm led to a slip of the tongue, giving away a crucial phrase prematurely.

Maurice E. Müller's way of thinking is uncommon and unique. Of course, there were others in the medical profession who worked and took notes as prolifically as he. And naturally there were those who, like Maurice E. Müller, were never satisfied with their work and tirelessly proposed new improvements and experiments that, seen individually, might appear unimpressive at first glance. Nevertheless, his particular skill at juggling a multitude of different ideas in his mind simultaneously is legendary. He can concentrate like no other. It is well known that, after a doze during a trip or sometimes even during a meeting, he can be expected upon waking to join in with a fresh idea without missing a beat.

Maurice E. Müller has always been quick to grasp the essential. It is no wonder that books on effective learning strategies piqued his particular interest. When he traveled to Ethiopia, the journey alone provided him with sufficient time to learn the basics of tropical medicine from a manual he had bought from a second-hand bookseller in Marseille. And, naturally, he had read Danis's presentation of osteosynthesis.[5] And yet it is amazing that his short stay of barely a day in Brussels was enough to convince him utterly of the Belgian surgeon's principles. As rumor will have it, Maurice E. Müller also mastered multiple sports disciplines after a brief but intense perusal of the right instructions. But those who know him well are keenly aware that quiet and unrelenting practice were indispensable to his success too, whether in wielding new instruments or performing magic tricks.

Merely understanding the essence of things has never satisfied Maurice E. Müller. He follows them through, considering all of their ramifications—and often with more patience than people looking for quick answers were willing to accept. Indeed, intellectual caution is to him part and parcel of the physician's duty. Thus he always took his time in testing methods and products before making them available to a wider public. For ten years he delved into and elaborated the principles of osteosynthesis, first alone and later with a very limited number of friends, before he allowed them to be disseminated widely. Similarly, he and Sir John Charnley agreed to limit strictly the testing of their techniques and hip implants to the very smallest of circles for the first six years.

Despite his great skill at the operating table, Maurice E. Müller has remained in awe of nature, always exercising the utmost respect. Not because of any mystical inclination, but rather on the insight that the sheer number of variables steering natural processes in the most diverse situations would always be able to take people, and physicians in particular, by surprise. His natural caution applies to everything that has more than one facet. From this follows his lifelong imperative to document continually and evaluate treatments objectively until they have proven to be reliable. This is something he has consistently demanded, promoted, and practiced. "Evidence-based medicine" may sound modern and critical, but it is nothing other than Maurice E. Müller's early call for operations and implants to be documented for as long a period as possible.

Readers of Danis or even of Lambotte, another Belgian orthopedist, who coined the term "osteosynthesis," were impressed by these physicians' case studies, accompanied as they were by thorough X-ray documentation. And it was Maurice E. Müller who subsequently was to systematize, perfect, and propagate this approach. For him it was an essential part of a surgeon's work and development, and it thus served as the organizing principle for the group of friends that was to become the Association for the Study of Internal Fixation (AO/ASIF)—an organization that revolutionized the treatment of fractures worldwide.[6]

Back then, the importance placed by Maurice E. Müller on obligatory, systematic, and long-term documentation did not gain wide acceptance. If it had, he reckons today, patients would have been spared many unnecessary complications. Not without bitterness he blames the industry and certain colleagues for their myopia in overlooking, or even knowingly tolerating, long-term side-effects for the sake of quickly conquering new markets. He himself kept long-term records whenever possible. As long as he called the shots in his company, Protek, careful documentation was part of its creed. And what is more, he used the millions of francs that came to him in the form of licenses to finance his foundations, which had as a top priority the promotion of careful record-keeping in medical practice. To this day, these investments provide funding for university appointments, institutes, and projects all over the world and have contributed to making the assessment of therapies systematic, objective, and verifiable by third parties. In nearly all lectures he has held since becoming professor emeritus, he has focused on the necessity of such documentation. This could be his legacy.

Many pioneers of osteosynthesis, including Lambotte and Danis, were solitary individuals. But Maurice E. Müller is different: because it was his intention to establish reliable techniques that would benefit many, he sought within his growing group of friends the expertise that would help him along his way. He often visited the operating theaters of fellow surgeons, for example. What he saw there only increased his interest in improving and expanding upon his techniques. He realized that he could not achieve the reliability he was seeking simply by making small improvements here and there. Moreover, he knew that his goal would require the development of entire systems in which individual elements followed a set of guiding principles. These individual elements included instruments, implants, materials, a wide variety of products, help for planning, instruction, and assistance in special cases. Education became the core element of this approach.

With conviction and throughout his entire life, Maurice E. Müller has selflessly passed on his knowledge, going far beyond his academic duties. Thanks to him, hands-on, comprehensive training by practicing physicians and a broad range of methods became a hallmark of AO/ASIF and its successors. These very first courses have remained especially fresh in the memories of those students who had the privilege of attending them. They knew they were experiencing, at first hand, crucial innovations in the field of practical surgery. Today, AO/ASIF seminars in Davos and courses specializing in hip surgery in Bern have spawned a generation of imitators all over the world. AO/ASIF textbooks have been translated into every language and have become the standard.[7]

Education also has another, deeper meaning for Maurice E. Müller, however. During his time in Africa, he became convinced that a doctor only really knows his subject if he is capable of successfully teaching it to others in a clear and competent manner. Teaching is for him a way to ensure that he has understood what he wants to say.

At first, the devices that Maurice E. Müller and his friends improved, modified, and invented were crafted by hand. It was long before modern industrial manufacturing came into it, and so small was the business that two rooms in his sister's apartment were entirely sufficient for both storage and distribution. But when they started to disseminate their ideas, it soon became clear that ensuring efficient production and consistent quality would require industrial methods and partners. Personal financial success did not, however, play a role. After covering costs, the proceeds were funneled into research, educa-tion, and development. AO/ASIF wanted doctors, not businessmen, to make the important decisions. In the technical commission that steered product development, medical and technical issues were the prevailing criteria and not those of profit or the market.

If a development made sense in the eyes of the surgeons, they did not worry about numbers.

Despite or perhaps because of these rules, after four decades these modest beginnings have been transformed into a range of businesses with worldwide presence. Today the net worth of all companies founded on these innovations—be they the original owners or simply imitators—is in the magnitude of tens of millions of Swiss francs—unimaginable for those who still remember the first lathes in Grenchen, Waldenburg, and Winterthur.

Without Maurice E. Müller, these companies, jobs, and values would not exist today. All along, financial gain, in and of itself, has been of no interest to him. He has not profited personally from his inventions or developments, for he donated his patents and instruments to AO/ASIF. He has retained the rights to inventions related to hip treatments, but in this matter as well, the lion's share went to his foundations. As he once wrote to Renzo Piano, "Money only acquires value from what one does with it and from the results that remain even years later."[8] When he finally sold the Protek corporation to Sulzer, he set a large amount of the proceeds aside for a project he knew would be worthwhile—an act his wife and children also supported.

And this is our cue to turn to the other founder: Martha Müller-Lüthi. Maurice E. Müller often said that he had his wife to thank for being able to pursue his dreams so consistently. She and Maurice met while he was performing his military service in Linden, near Oberdiessbach. Her resolute manner made an immediate impression on him. Yet she was rather irresolute at that time: he ws a handsome man, but of course there were also officers, and she had no way of knowing that the patrolman would become a major. When he called her out of the blue in 1946 to ask if she would follow him to Ethiopia, where a Swiss team of surgeons was to build new medical care facilities, she accepted and married him there. Maurice E. Müller remarked with a hint of irony, "Maybe she only said yes because of Africa."

From the first day in Ethiopia, Martha Müller-Lüthi realized that she would often have to wait patiently at the side of a physician who was devoting his life to his career. When she finally landed in Ethiopia after a long trip and months of separation, before even greeting her, Maurice E. Müller first had to discuss with a colleague detailed arrangements for the delivery of new mattresses to the hospital. Ever since that day, Martha Müller-Lüthi, like so many women of her genera-tion, has unconditionally accepted the responsibilities of a wife and mother, standing by a ceaselessly busy man. While he was busy with operations, travel, and research, she took care of house and hearth. She infused life into the home on Melchenbühlweg that she had had built. She looked after her husband, their three children, and the sizeable bundle of grandchildren to come—and last but not least, made welcome their friends and guests. Maurice E. Müller could, and indeed did, rely on her entirely. Once, when he sent his bank a payment authorization, they flat out denied his request because they were only familiar with his wife's signature.

Martha gradually began to create her own world with her own projects. She surrounded herself with architecture and architects, with art and artists, music and musicians.

In 1968, Martha Müller-Lüthi discovered the plot of land, bordering the Schöngrün area, on which the family house is now situated. In her customary way, she won over the owner, despite a long list of interested buyers who had gotten there sooner. "Well then, why don't you just reverse the order of the list?" she asked. Years later, one of the Müller family's foundations bought the adjacent property with the proceeds from Protek licenses. From that point on Schöngrün's development, its architecture, and the accompanying plans and obstacles became a frequent topic of conversation between the couple and other members of their family.

As Martha was making preparations for her husband's eightieth birthday in 1998, she managed to secure the pianist Maurizio Pollini, whose ability to play had been restored years before by Maurice E. Müller, as the leading celebrity of the birthday concert. When it came to finding a venue, Martha had to content herself with the Hodler-Saal in the Kunstmuseum Bern, despite its acoustics. As luck would have it, the room had to be vacated immediately following the concert for a public discussion of the Klee collection's imperiled future in Bern—a discussion that was to spur public and political discourse on the matter. As Martha and Maurice E. Müller recount, it was not until this day that they realized the city might lose these wonderful paintings forever. Martha Müller-Lüthi had already shown an interest in Renzo Piano's museum designs for quite some time, and both she and her husband had already considered establishing a museum foundation, albeit without yet knowing what its particular mission would be. Be that as it may, immediately following the birthday concert in the museum, Martha and Maurice decided to what ends they would allocate the funds they had set aside, and what would eventually take shape in the center of Schöngrün: the Zentrum Paul Klee. At Martha's initiative, the Zentrum plans were later expanded to include a concert hall for performances by noteworthy artists.

It may be sheer serendipity that Paul Klee's final resting place lies just a few steps away from the new center which carries his name—a place where visitors will be able to marvel at his works and artistic worlds, and where Maurice E. Müller and his family have lived for many years. But perhaps one cannot put everything down to chance. In any event, the parallels between the lives of the artist Paul Klee and the physician Maurice E. Müller are striking. The achievements of both men hang on an extraordinary interplay of craftsmanship and intellect. Both Müller and Klee are similar in their inexhaustible and lifelong commitment to the paths they chose to follow in their early years. Each man knew that he wanted to, and would, achieve something completely new and unexpected in his respective area of endeavor. From the beginning to the end of their careers, both men kept meticulous records of their work—not out of egotism, but rather because they wanted to know how their thoughts, abilities, and knowledge changed over time, and what resulted from these changes. And finally, both men had not just a vision but also the ability to translate their dreams into works of art or medical practice. And in this way, both men changed their world.

1 See Maurice E. Müller, "Klee-Museum, meine Vision" (manuscript, September 22, 1998).
2 Manuscript by Chadwick F. Smith, August 24, 2002.
3 See Urs Heim, Das Phänomen ao (Bern, 2001), p. 26.
4 See Maurice E. Müller, "George Perkins Lecture" (manuscript, October 1, 1971).
5 Robert Danis, Technique de l'ostéosynthèse (Paris, 1932) and Théorie et pratique de l'ostéosynthèse (Paris, 1949).
6 On the history of AO/ASIF, see Heim, Das Phänomen ao (see note 3).
7 See especially Maurice. E. Müller et al., Manual of Internal Fixation, 3rd ed. (Berlin, 1991).
8 Maurice E. Müller to Renzo Piano, January 20, 2003.

Biography of Renzo Piano

Renzo Piano was born in Genoa, Italy, on September 14, 1937.
He graduated in 1964 from the School of Architecture of Milan Polytechnic. As a student, he worked under the guidance of the designer-architect Franco Albini, while also regularly attending his father's building sites where he gained valuable practical experience.
Between 1965 and 1970, he completed his education and gained further work experience with study trips to Britain and the United States. It was at this time that he met Jean Prouvé. They formed a friendship that would have a profound influence on Piano's professional life.
In 1971, he founded the "Piano & Rogers" agency together with Richard Rogers, his partner on the Centre Pompidou project in Paris. This was followed in 1977 by the founding of "l'Atelier Piano & Rice" along with the engineer Peter Rice, who would work with him on many projects until Rice's death in 1993.
He then founded the Renzo Piano Building Workshop, with offices in Paris and Genoa. His approximately 100 staff (who include architects, engineers, and other specialists) work in close collaboration with a number of associated architects, with whom Piano has maintained professional links for many years.

Projects

1964
Lightweight structures

1969
Italian Industry Pavilion at the 1970 Expo, Osaka, Japan

1973
Office building for B&B, Como, Italy

1974
Single-family homes, Cusago, Milan, Italy

1977
Centre Georges Pompidou, Paris, France (with Richard Rogers)
IRCAM, Institute for Acoustic Research, Paris, France

1979
Participation in a project to restore historic centers, Otranto, Italy

1980
VSS experimental vehicle for FIAT, Turin, Italy

1982
Apartments in the Rigo district of Perugia, Italy
Alexander Calder retrospective, exhibition architecture, Turin, Italy

1984
Conversion of Schlumberger factory buildings, Paris, France
Auditorium for the performance of the opera "Prometeo" by Luigi Nono, Venice, Italy
Office building for Olivetti, Naples, Italy

1985
Lowara office building, Vicenza, Italy

1986
IBM pavilion for travelling exhibition in Europe

1987
Museum for the Menil Collection, Houston, USA
Building for Light Metals Experimental Institute, Novara, Italy

1990
Soccer stadium, San Nicola, Bari, Italy
Shopping center, Bercy 2, Paris, France
IRCAM extension, Paris, France

1991
"Crown Princess" and "Regal Princess" cruise ships for P&O, USA, Monfalcone Shipyard, Trieste, Italy
Housing for the city of Paris, Rue de Meaux, Paris, France
Thomson Optronics factory, Saint-Quentin-en-Yvelines, France
Renzo Piano Building Workshop, Punta Nave, Genoa, Italy
Subway stations, Genoa, Italy

1992
Headquarters for the Credito Industriale Sardo bank, Cagliari, Sardinia, Italy
Columbus International Exposition, Aquarium and Congress Hall, 1992, Genoa, Italy

1994
Kansai International Airport Terminal, Osaka, Japan
Renzo Piano Building Workshop Office, Genoa, Italy
Auditorium Parco della Musica, hall with 2,800 seats, Rome, Italy

1995
Cy Twombly Pavilion, Houston, USA
Meridien Hotel and business center in the Lingotto district, Turin, Italy
Headquarters of the harbor authorities, Genoa, Italy

1996
Cité Internationale — cinema, offices, Museum of Modern Art, congress center (200, 800, and 300 seats), park, Lyon, France
I Portici (shopping street in the Lingotto district), Turin, Italy
Ushibuka Bridge, Kumamoto, Japan

1997
Reconstruction of the Atelier Brancusi, Paris, France
NEMO, Museum of Science and Technology, Amsterdam, The Netherlands
Fondation Beyeler Museum, Riehen, Basle, Switzerland
The Debis building, headquarters of DaimlerChrysler, Potsdamer Platz, Berlin, Germany
Harvard University Art Museum, master plan, renovation and expansion project, Cambridge, Mass., USA

1998
Wind tunnel for Ferrari, Maranello, Modena, Italy
Jean-Marie Tjibaou Cultural Center, Nouméa, New Caledonia
DaimlerChrysler Design Center, Sindelfingen, Germany
DaimlerChrysler projects on Potsdamer Platz: musical theater, Imax cinema, apartments, retail stores, Berlin, Germany
Lodi Bank Headquarters, Lodi, Italy
Lingotto Phase 3 (university, art gallery), Turin, Italy

1999
Hotel and casino, Cité Internationale, Lyon, France
Restoration and expansion of the Old Harbor, Genoa, Italy
Shopping and offices center, Lecco, Italy
Woodruff Arts Center extension, Atlanta, USA
Fondation Beyeler extension, Riehen, Basle, Switzerland

2000
Interior and exterior restoration of the Centre Pompidou, Paris, France
B1 Office tower on Potsdamer Platz, Berlin, Germany
KPN Telecom office tower, Rotterdam, The Netherlands
Aurora Place, office tower and apartment blocks, Sydney, Australia
New headquarters of Virgin Continental Europe, Paris, France
Reconstruction of Genoa's Old Harbor for the G8 summit, Genoa, Italy

2001
Auditorium of the Banca Popolare di Lodi, Lodi, Italy
Maison Hermès, Tokyo, Japan
Niccolo' Paganini Auditorium, Parma, Italy
Exhibition structure, realized for the G8 summit, Genoa, Italy
University campus, Preganziol, Treviso, Italy

2002
"Parco della Musica" Auditorium, 700 and 1200-seat halls, Rome, Italy
Multiplex movie theater in Lingotto, Turin, Italy
Pinacoteca Giovanni e Marella Agnelli in Lingotto, Turin, Italy

2003

Nasher Scuplture Center, Dallas, USA
Congress and concert hall in Lingotto, Turin, Italy

2004

Padre Pio Pilgrimage Church, San Giovanni Rotondo, Foggia, Italy
Headquarters of the newspaper Il Sole 24 Ore, Milan, Italy
New headquarters of EMI Musique France, Paris, France

2005

Zentrum Paul Klee, Bern, Switzerland
Peek & Cloppenburg department store, Cologne, Germany
High Museum of Art extension, Atlanta, USA

Current Projects (2005)

Business, leisure, and service center, Nola, Naples, Italy
Capuchin Monastery, San Giovanni Rotondo, Foggia, Italy
New subway stations, Genoa, Italy
Art Institute of Chicago extension, Chicago, USA
Braço de Prata housing complex, Lisbon, Portugal
Museum of Modern Art, Sarajevo, Bosnia
California Academy of Sciences extension, San Francisco, USA
Congress center, Cité Internationale, Lyon, France
London Bridge Tower, London, England
The New York Times building, NY, USA
The Morgan Library extension, NY, USA
Office and apartment block, Saint Giles Court, London, England
La Rocca Winery, Grosseto, Italy
Restoration of the old Michelin factory site, Trento, Italy
Columbia University, campus plan, New York, USA
Los Angeles County Museum, Lacma, Los Angeles, USA
Whitney Museum extension, New York, USA
Isabella Stewart Gardner Museum extension, Boston, USA
Restoration of the old Falck site, Sesto San Giovanni, Italy
New London Bridge House, London, England

Prizes and Honors

1978

Union Internationale des Architects Honorary Fellowship, Mexico City, Mexico

1981

Compasso d'Oro award, Milan, Italy
AIA Honorary Fellowship, USA

1984

Commandeur des Arts et des Lettres award, Paris, France

1985

Légion d'Honneur, Paris, France
R.I.B.A. Honorary Fellowship, Britain

1989

R.I.B.A. Royal Gold Medal for Architecture, Britain
Cavaliere di Gran Croce award, Italy

1990
Honorary doctorate, University of Stuttgart, Germany
Kyoto Prize of the Inamori Foundation, Kyoto, Japan

1991
Richard Neutra Prize, Pomona, California, USA

1992
Honorary doctorate, University of Delft, The Netherlands

1993
American Academy of Arts and Sciences, Fellow, London, England

1994
American Academy of Arts and Letters, Honorary Fellowship, USA
Arnold W. Brunner Memorial Prize, USA
Chevalier, l'Ordre National du Mérite, France
UNESCO Goodwill Ambassador for Architecture
Premio Michelangelo, Italy
Prize for Actuactiones temporales de Urbanismo y Arquitectura from the Ayuntamiento de Madrid, Spain

1995
Art prize of the Akademie der Künste, Berlin, Germany
Praemium Imperiale, Japan
Erasmus Prize, The Netherlands

1996
Premio Capo Circeo, Italy

1998
Pritzker Architecture Prize, USA

1999
Architect of the National Academy of San Luca , Rome, Italy

2000
Officier, Ordre National de la Légion d'Honneur, France
Leone d'Oro, Venice, Italy
Spirit of Nature Wood Architecture Award, Finland
Premio Leonardo, Italy

2001
Wexner Prize, Wexner Center for the Arts, Columbus, Ohio, USA.

2002
Honorary doctorate, Pratt Institute, New York, USA
Médaille D'Or, International Union of Architects, Berlin
Michelangelo Antonioni for the Arts, Italy

2003
Gold Medal, Italian Architecture Triennale, Milan, Italy
Prize "Una vita nella musica—Artur Rubinstein," Venice, Italy

2004
Grifo d'oro, Comune di Genova, Genoa, Italy
2003 Culture prize of the Italian-American Chamber of Commerce and Industry, New York, USA

2005
McKim Prize, American Academy in Rome

This catalogue is published in conjunction with the opening of the Zentrum Paul Klee, Bern, June 20, 2005.

Issued by
Zentrum Paul Klee, Bern

Editorial direction
Ursina Barandun and Nathalie Gygax Huber

Copyediting
Melanie Newton

Translations
Amanda Crain

Graphic design and typesetting
Atelier Sternstein, Stuttgart

Typeface
FF DIN

Paper
Printed on Furioso 150 g/m² from m-real, Biberist, Switzerland

Binding
G. Lachenmeier, Realwerk, Reutlingen

Reproductions and printing by
Dr. Cantz'sche Druckerei, Ostfildern

Published by
Hatje Cantz Verlag
Zeppelinstrasse 32
73760 Ostfildern
Germany

Tel. +49 711 4405-0
Fax +49 711 4405-220
www.hatjecantz.com

Hatje Cantz books are available internationally at selected bookstores and from the following distribution partners:
USA/North America – D.A.P., Distributed Art Publishers, New York, www.artbook.com
UK – Art Books International, London, www.art-bks.com
Australia – Towerbooks, French Forest (Sydney), www.towerbks.com.au
France – Interart, Paris, www.interart.fr
Belgium – Exhibitions International, Leuven, www.exhibitionsinternational.be
Switzerland – Scheidegger, Affoltern am Albis, www.ava.ch

For Asia, Japan, South America, and Africa, as well as for general questions, please contact Hatje Cantz directly at sales@hatjecantz.de, or visit our homepage www.hatjecantz.com for further information.

ISBN-10: 3-7757-1550-9
ISBN-13: 978-3-7757-1550-8
Trade edition: Hardcover with dust jacket
Museum edition: Hardcover

This catalogue is also available in German and French
ISBN-10: 3-7757-1549-4;
ISBN-13: 978-3-7757-1549-2 (German)
ISBN-10: 3-7757-1551-7;
ISBN-13: 978-3-7757-1551-5 (French)

Printed in Germany

Front cover photo
Dominique Uldry, Bern

Zentrum Paul Klee
Monument im Fruchtland 3
3006 Bern
Switzerland

Tel. +41 31 359 01 01
Fax +41 31 359 01 02
www.zpk.org

Photo Credits

Renzo Piano Building Workshop, Genoa and Paris:
pp. 1–2, 15–17, 19, 23–27, 28 (top), 31, 34, 37, 42, 44–57

Dominique Uldry, Bern:
Cover and pp. 10–11, 13, 22, 28 (bottom), 29–30, 32–33, 35–36, 38–40, 58–67, 72–143

Peter von Gunten, Bern:
pp. 14, 41

Unknown photographer, Zentrum Paul Klee, Bern, Klee Family Donation:
p. 21 (top)

Felix Klee, Zentrum Paul Klee, Bern, Klee Family Donation:
p. 20 (top)

Lily Klee, Zentrum Paul Klee, Bern, Klee Family Donation:
p. 20 (bottom)

Hansueli Trachsel, Bern:
p. 21 (bottom)

Jens-Erik Nielsen, private collection, Bern:
p. 21 (center)